The Life and Times of
VICTORIA

OVERLEAF LEFT Princess Victoria
by Westall, painted when she
was eleven years old.
OVERLEAF RIGHT Cardboard box,
consisting of six partitions, each
with a top decorated by Victoria's
portrait. This is one of Victoria's
possessions from Kensington Palace.
Judging from the style of the portrait, the
Princess must have been about fourteen
when the box was made for her.

The Life and Times of

VICTORIA

Dorothy Marshall

Introduction by Antonia Fraser

WELCOME RAIN

NEW YORK

Additional titles in the **Life and Times** series,
published under the General Editorship of Antonia Fraser include:

Elizabeth I by Neville Williams (1-56649-198-3)
Henry VIII by Robert Lacey (1-56649-199-1)
Richard III by Anthony Cheetham (1-56649-038-3)

First WELCOME RAIN edition 1998
Published by WELCOME RAIN
New York, New York

First published in 1972 by
Weidenfeld & Nicolson
An imprint of the Orion Publishing Group
Orion House, 5 Upper St Martin's Lane
London WC2H 9EA

ISBN 1-56649-036-7
M 10 9 8 7 6 5 4 3 2 1

© George Weidenfeld
and Nicolson Limited
and Book Club
Associates 1972

Series designed by Paul Watkins
Layout by Juanita Grout

Filmset by Keyspools Limited, Golborne, Lancs
Printed in Great Britain by
Butler & Tanner Ltd, Frome and London

Contents

Introduction

BRITAIN HAS BEEN GRACED by only six Queens regnant – from the somewhat shadowy figure of Matilda, down to our own sovereign, the second Elizabeth. It is a situation which can fairly claim to be intriguing from the start: the contrast between the august office and the theoretically fragile occupant. And it is indeed this very contrast which often constitutes the monarch's major problem, when a Queen who is also a woman must face the demands of both roles and try to reconcile them. It is a question to which several different solutions have been found, from the uxorious submission of William's Mary to the successful celibacy of Elizabeth I. But it was during the incredible sixty-four-year-long span of Victoria's reign that the problem was illuminated with most theatrical and absorbing effect. Not only was Victoria herself a supremely feminine creature – no shades here of Cecil's Elizabeth who was 'something less than a woman' – but as a loving if tempestuous wife to Albert, the mother of nine children, she alone of our reigning Queens, until the present day, found herself actually coping with the coincidental problems of royal family life and conscientious government. It must be remembered that Mary Tudor's efforts at child-bearing were fruitless, and Queen Anne was cursed with an inability to produce children that survived. Only Victoria had to combine in effect the needs of the nursery with the cares of office. As Dorothy Marshall writes: 'In some ways Victoria is the forerunner of the modern career woman, dovetailing the role of devoted wife and mother with that of chief consultant to a large international concern.'

But of course, quite independent of her own personality, Victoria happened to come to the throne in time to preside over a momentous period in our history. The extraordinary change over the face of Britain incumbent in the spread of the Industrial Revolution is most effectively illustrated by the rise in population: a country which contained nine millions in 1801, and eighteen millions in 1851, encompassed over thirty millions at the time of Victoria's death in 1901. And this hardly takes into account the twists and turns of British diplomacy, the crystallisation of the theory of Empire, and the profound changes in social life. As it is, Dorothy Marshall neatly weaves the dramatic personal facets of Victoria's story into the tapestry of nineteenth-century Britain: her pride in 'her dear soldiers' is seen against the background of the Crimean War, which made great army organisation necessary. Her widely differing relationships with her Prime Ministers, from the beloved Lord Melbourne of the early years, to the equally loved Disraeli of the later period, including less satisfactory terms with the unquenchable Palmerston and Mr Gladstone, are all part of the development of the constitutional proprieties of Crown and Government.

Dorothy Marshall indeed sees Victoria as one who, throughout her life, sought in her relationships, from her uncle King Leopold down to the controversial Highland servant John Brown, what we should now term as some kind of 'father figure'. At the same time her country was coming to demand from its sovereign as of right some sort of symbolic yet active representation, possibly even a 'mother figure'. In the balance between these two needs, those of a sensitive woman and a great country, lies the fascinating material for Dorothy Marshall's wise and perceptive study.

Antonia Fraser

Acknowledgments

Photographs and illustrations were supplied by or are reproduced by kind permission of the following. The pictures on pages *2, 3, 14,* 18/1, 18/2, 21, 25, 28, 37, 38, 45, 47, *50–1, 62–3,* 69, 74, 78/2, 81, 82/1, 82/2, 84, 101, *116/1, 116/2, 125, 129,* 131, 132, 133/1, 133/2, 146–7, 148, 150–1, 155, 156, 160, 161, 166–7, 186, 204, 204–5 are reproduced by gracious permission of H.M. the Queen. Aerofilms: 158; Nicholas Bentley: 201; Gordon Barnes: 198/1; British Museum: 10–11, 13, 16/2, 47, 48, 58–9, 69, 88–9, 93, 100, 106, 121, 126, 163, 177, 181, 182, 191; British Railway Board: 136/2; Clapham Museum of Transport: 136/1; John Curtis: *194;* Department of Environment (Crown Copyright): 212; John Freeman: 13, 104; Gernsheim Collection: 71, 78/1, 188–9, 215; Guildhall Library: 42, 109/2, *113/1, 113/2, 195,* 198/2, 200/2, *206–7;* Illustrated London News: 79, 96/1, 96/2, 111/2, 114, 137, 138, 140, 141, 144, 170–1; A. F. Kersting: 159; Mander and Mitchenson Theatre Collection: 80; Mansell Collection: 115; National Monuments Record: 198/1; National Portrait Gallery: 16/1, 41, 54, 61, 92, 105, 109, 111/1, 178/2, 183/1, 183/2; Executors of Sir William Nicholson: 214; Radio Times Hulton Picture Library: 91, 116, 123, 178/1, 208, 213/1; Royal Institute of British Architects: 142, 143/1, 143/2; Salvation Army: 200/1, 201; Science Museum: 22–3, 23/1, 23/2; Edwin Smith: 136/1; Tate Gallery: *15;* Trades Union Congress Library: 97; Penny Tweedie: 183/3; Victoria and Albert Museum: 34–5, 174, 216–7; Margaret Willes: 213/2; Derek Witty: 169.

The author owes acknowledgment to the following for quotations: Roger Fulford, *Dearest Child* (1964), and *Dearest Maria* (1966), Evans Bros Ltd; George Earle Buckle, *Letters of Queen Victoria,* series two and three, John Murray (Publishers) Ltd.

Picture research by Gillian Mounsey.

REGENCY ————

Pub July 8 1830 by J. McLean 26 Haymarket London

THE LIFE OF QUEEN VICTORIA has a triple interest; it combines the study of a forceful character with that of Victorian womanhood and of a great and successful monarch. In some ways Victoria is the forerunner of the modern career woman, dovetailing the role of devoted wife and mother with that of chief consultant to a large international concern, which grew steadily in its resources and magnitude throughout the years of her stewardship. Moreover this dual role had to be lived in the fierce light of national publicity. Victoria had to be at once a wife, a mother and a queen. This is the dilemma that provides the vital thread through the labyrinth of her life. Fortunately, helping her to sustain both roles, Victoria was buoyed up with a steady belief in her own judgment to discern right from wrong. She was a singularly honest person and is reported to have once declared that expediency was a word which had no meaning for her. As a result, she saw people and problems in black and white; indecision was never allowed to blunt the edge of her determination.

Victoria was born into a world of change and conflict. Britain was still feeling the results of her long struggle with first Revolutionary and then Napoleonic France. In the North and Midlands the tentacles of the new industrialism were extending every year, as new cotton mills were built and new blast furnaces poured out mass-produced iron. The population appeared to be increasing at an uncontrollable rate, augmenting the misery of unemployment which the post-war depression had caused the workers in these new industries. Under new pressures even the traditional structure of society itself was crumbling. Men no longer thought in terms of 'order and degree' based on birth, but on class, with its underlying economic connotations, as a measure of a person's place in society. Even the moral values on which that society was based were changing as the new forces were challenging and driving underground the accepted standards of the past. On the one hand there was the licentious tradition of the Regency – both the future William IV and Victoria's own father lived openly with their mistresses, the actress Mrs Jordan and Madame St Laurent respectively. On the other hand there was the new seriousness of the Evangelical movement, compounded of a genuine religious feeling and a conviction that if society were to survive the

PREVIOUS PAGES Cartoon of 1830 by William Heath, satirising Leopold's plan to create a rival court around Victoria, with the Duchess of Kent as Regent. Leopold is shown with Princess Victoria upon his knee, while her mother looks on from the throne. In the background Wellington addresses the Council.

distress and discontent of a war and post-war years the ruling classes must set an example to the lower orders. George IV remained an unrepentant *roué* to the end of his days, but circumstances combined to push both the Duke of Clarence and the Duke of Kent into the ranks of domestic respectability. Something of the same conflict is to be seen in Victoria herself. Though the term 'Victorian' has come to stand for a strict and even prudish morality, the young Victoria craved for pleasure and for gaiety. She was fortunate in her mentors and in her marriage, otherwise with her affectionate, emotional nature she might well never have come to stand for all that was most respectable in nineteenth-century womanhood!

Queen Victoria was born on 24 May 1819 at Kensington Palace – her Coburg grandmother called her the 'May Flower' but the reason for her birth had been political not romantic. On 6 November 1817 the only daughter of the Prince Regent, Charlotte, the wife of Leopold of Saxe-Coburg, died in childbirth. It was unlikely that the Regent would have other legitimate children. His repugnance to his wife Caroline was such that co-habitation had ceased many years earlier; indeed, after

he came to the throne as George IV, he tried, unsuccessfully, to divorce her. Yet, unless Caroline died, so enabling the Regent to marry again, there was no hope that he might leave a legitimate heir to succeed him. Only two of his brothers, the Dukes of York and Cumberland, were married, and they had no legitimate heirs, so there followed a flurry of diplomatic activity to provide the rest with brides. William, Duke of Clarence, married Adelaide of Saxe-Meiningen, Adolphus, Duke of Cambridge, married Augusta of Hesse-Cassel, while the bereaved Prince Leopold of Saxe-Coburg had the satisfaction of seeing his sister, the widowed Princess of Leiningen married

LEFT Princess Charlotte, only daughter of George IV and heir apparent to the throne, was married to Prince Leopold of Saxe-Coburg in May 1816. This painting shows Charlotte and Leopold at Covent Garden.

BELOW Charlotte's sudden death caused upheavals in the royal family and there followed an undignified rush amongst the Regent's unmarried brothers to find wives. The Dukes of Clarence, Cambridge and Kent all married in 1818. This cartoon was published in April 1819 and shows on the left, Clarence and Adelaide of Saxe-Meiningen, whose children all died in infancy; in the centre, Cambridge and Augusta of Hesse-Cassel with their son George; and to the right, Kent with Victoria of Leiningen, heavily pregnant, whose child would exclude Cambridge's heir from the succession; and Cumberland who had produced no legitimate child as yet.

to the Duke of Kent. As Victoria was later to observe of her uncle 'he is ever ready and ever *most able* to assist his family'. Two years later, a mere eight months after his daughter's birth, the Duke of Kent died, leaving a minute income of less than £300 from a jointure to his widowed Duchess.

Without the help of her brother Leopold, who was still living in England at Claremont, the Duchess would have fared badly. Nobody as yet saw a future queen in her infant daughter, Alexandrina Victoria, because it was expected that the Duke of Clarence, now heir to the throne after the accession of the Regent in 1820, would have children. This was a reasonable assumption as he already had a large brood of illegitimate children and his legal wife was young. However, none of his legitimate children survived infancy, his last daughter dying in 1821. Therefore, until 1825 when Parliament, in recognition of the fact that Victoria must now be regarded as William IV's probable successor, voted the Duchess an annuity of £6,000 for the maintenance and education of her daughter, both mother and child were dependent on the allowance that Leopold made them. This he was well able to afford, as on his marriage to Princess Charlotte, Parliament had voted him an annuity of £50,000. The widow and her daughter lived very simply in rooms assigned to them in Kensington Palace, with a routine varied by visits in the summer to Ramsgate or to Claremont. Their contacts with the Court were few. There had been no love lost between the Regent and the Duke of Kent and it was not until 1826 that Victoria and her mother were invited to stay at Cumberland Lodge when the King was at Royal Lodge, Windsor. Gouty and paint-raddled as George IV was, enough of his old charm remained to make an impression on his little niece, to whom he gave his portrait set in diamonds, which Lady Conyngham pinned on her shoulder. From Victoria's point of view, in spite of having to kiss her uncle, the visit was an enjoyable one, particularly when she was driven round Virginia Water in the royal phaeton and taken aboard a barge from which the party fished, while on a neighbouring one a band played. The visit was repeated in the following year, but, alas, 'it rained dreadfully'.

Of William IV, Victoria's memories were less happy, largely because by then she was old enough to be conscious of the

LEFT Edward, Duke of Kent, who died less than eight months after his daughter's birth: portrait by George Dawe, 1818.

RIGHT Victoria's uncle, William IV, whose relationship with her mother was always strained. As Victoria wrote later: 'he was odd, very odd and singular but his intentions were often ill interpreted'. Painting by Sir Martin Archer-Shee, 1833.
child as of yet.

strain that existed between him and her mother. William himself, though eccentric, was a friendly person, anxious to show his favour towards his niece. Victoria later wrote of him 'He was always kind to me and he *meant* it well I know. I am grateful for it and shall always remember his kindness with gratitude. He was odd, very odd and singular, but his intentions were often ill interpreted.' Moreover, his wife, Queen Adelaide, who was, rather surprisingly, deeply attached to her elderly and bulbous-eyed husband, was a singularly sweet person. In the years before her husband's accession, she had made a happy home at Bushey for his children by Mrs Jordan without either comment or complaint. This was indeed part of the trouble, for the Duchess of Kent was perhaps over-conscious of her position as the mother of a future queen and as such was determined to protect her daughter from every contaminating influence. She found it deeply shocking that a man should openly acknowledge his bastards, though in fact the Court under William and Adelaide was almost bourgeois in its respectability. Nevertheless the Duchess kept her daughter away from it as much as she could, even trumping up an excuse to prevent Victoria from attending her uncle's coronation. Behind this display of prudery there were deeper, half-unconscious motives for the Duchess's action. During the early years of her widowhood, she had resented the neglect with which she had been treated and the lack of support that she had received from the royal family. Moreover this resentment had been fanned by a man who had strong and unfortunate influence over her: Sir John Conroy, the Comptroller of her Household. He had been her husband's equerry, and the Duke had made him one of the executors of his will. Of Anglo-Irish descent, Conroy had a certain brash charm, though most of his contemporaries found him essentially vulgar and his manner with women too familiar. However, both Victoria's mother and her aunt, the Princess Sophia, who also had apartments in Kensington Palace, relied on him implicitly. This was unfortunate. Conroy was a man of considerable ambition who hoped to use his influence over the Duchess to carve out for himself a successful career as the power behind the throne, if William IV should die before Victoria reached her majority. It was therefore his policy that Victoria and her mother should be isolated from everyone who could hinder these plans. There is little doubt that Conroy used his influence to intensify the strain between the Duchess and the Court.

His plan seems to have been to follow the age-long Hanoverian precedent of building up a rival Court round the heir to the throne. One method was to institute a kind of royal progress to show Victoria (and even more her mother, as a possible Regent) to the people of England. Accordingly from 1832, when Victoria was thirteen, a series of visits to the great houses of such peers as were not firmly attached to the Court was arranged. There were benefits to Victoria's education in such tours. If her mother's attitude denied to her daughter the familiarity with Court life and the duties that would subsequently be hers, she did at least gain some knowledge of the country over which she was to rule. Nevertheless, except in a purely geographical sense, it was a limited knowledge. Victoria became acquainted with the life of the great country houses and with the pattern of aristocratic living, but she saw little of that of the mass of the people, except what could be observed along the roads over which their coach travelled or at the inns at which occasionally they were forced to stop for the night. It was on her first tour that she caught a glimpse of the new industrial nation which by the end of her life was to overtake the England of the coaching era to which her early journeys belonged. After changing horses at Birmingham, the young traveller commented in her journal on 'an extraordinary building flaming with fire' and that 'the country continues black, engines flaming, coals, in abundance everywhere smoking and burning coal heaps, intermingled with wretched huts and carts and little ragged children'.

These semi-royal progresses aroused William IV to fury, because the Duchess contrived that wherever they went they were received by the local dignitaries with addresses and demonstrations of loyalty. When the party lunched at Shrewsbury on their way to Welshpool, the Mayor presented the young Princess with a silver-topped oaken box filled with Shrewsbury cakes. When they arrived at Welshpool they were escorted into the town, which was decorated with 'arches, branches, flowers, flags, ribbons etc,' by a troop of Yeomanry. Finally, as they entered the park they were greeted by a salute of guns. To the King any salute of guns, with its aura of a royal progress, was the last straw, and he angrily ordered that it should be discontinued. The final breach between him and the Duchess seems to have been caused by her having extended and improved her suite at Kensington Palace without having first obtained the royal consent, though this may have been the result of a misunderstanding. The occasion for a public explosion was a banquet given by William IV on his birthday, at which he attacked the Duchess personally by declaring that his one fear was that he might die before his niece came of age and that in consequence the Regency might fall into the hands of 'a person sitting near me who is surrounded by evil advisers and who is incompetent to act with propriety in the position in which she would be placed'. Not surprisingly the Duchess was

Victoria's drawing of herself after she had contracted typhoid at Ramsgate in October 1835.

frozen into speechless indignation and poor Victoria burst into tears, which in moments of emotion she was always prone to do.

Nevertheless it is probable that in her heart Victoria agreed with her uncle, at least in thinking that her mother was surrounded by evil advisers who intended to use the Regency, if it occurred, for their own advancement. By now she had received ample proof of this, and her detestation of Sir John Conroy was deep and lasting. In the October of 1835 she had contracted typhoid at Ramsgate, and for the rest of the month had been desperately ill. While she was still weak and convalescent, Sir John, abetted by the Duchess, had tried to wring a signed promise from Victoria that when she became Queen she would appoint him to the key position of her private secretary. Somehow, as she told Lord Melbourne later, she found the strength and determination to refuse. The forlorn misery that she endured then was an experience that for years she could neither forgive nor forget. It embittered her relations with her mother and left her with no liking for her mother's lady-in-waiting, Lady Flora Hastings, a fact which was later to have disastrous consequences for them both. This coldness is apparent in her

The Stockton and Darlington Railway

In 1814, George Stephenson built his first locomotive, and four years later suggested that steam locomotives should be used on the projected railway from Stockton to Darlington. This was opened on 27 September 1825, and was the first public passenger railway in the world. The single-track line, with passing places every quarter mile, was thirty-eight miles long, and Stephenson himself drove the first train from Brusselton to Stockton.

RIGHT Photographs of the pioneers of the Stockton and Darlington Railway, together with their locomotives and advertisements. In the centre is the first engine employed on the line.

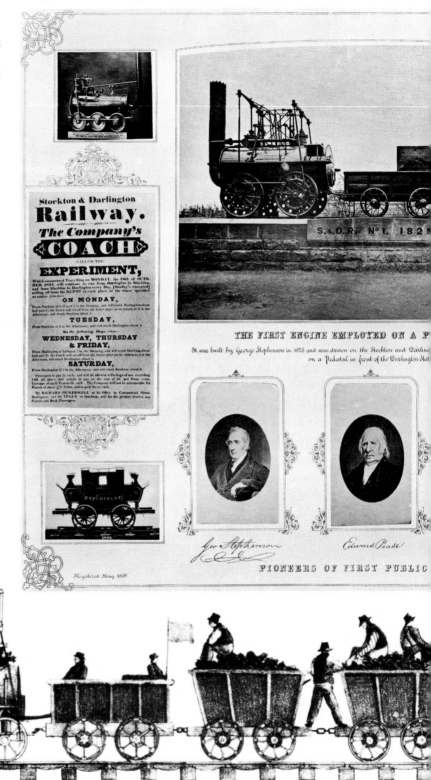

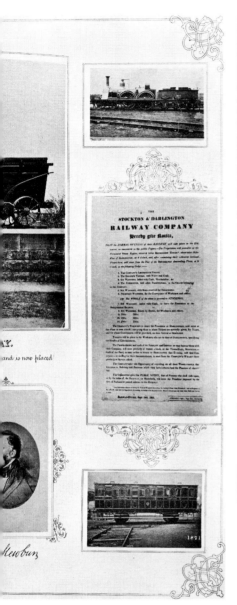

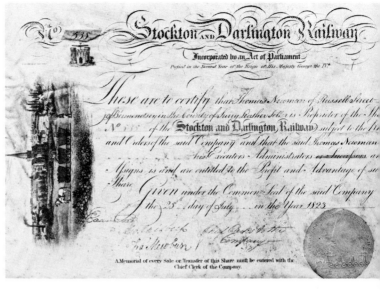

Train of Waggons crossing the Turnpike Road near Darlington.

TOP RIGHT A share
certificate dated 25 July
1823 for the Stockton
and Darlington
Railway Company.

ABOVE AND BELOW
The opening ceremony
of the Stockton and
Darlington Railway in
September 1825, and the
first train.

journal, which her mother had given to Victoria on her thirteenth birthday so that she could keep a record of their coming visit to Wales. It was fortunate for future historians that the habit begun then of writing up the events of the day persisted throughout her life, thus providing invaluable clues to her immediate reactions to events as they happened.

Until she became Queen, this journal must be used with a realisation of its limitations. It was not a secret diary; her mother and her governess saw it regularly and young Victoria learned to practise the wisdom of keeping her thoughts to herself when these were critical of the people round her. She confined herself to a meticulous account of her daily doings, of such subjects as where on their journeys they changed horses, descriptions of the places where they stayed, the names of the people they met, and later the books that she read, or the concerts she attended. Her personal opinions were confined to such subjects and from them the historian can discover who were her favourite singers, actors or authors. There is no mention of the jealousies and pressures which later made her describe her childhood as a sad one. Even the final tussle with Conroy, with all the resentment and bitterness that it caused, was never recorded. In her early journals it is the omissions that give the best clues to Victoria's private feelings. She was affectionate in an age when emotion and sensibility were appropriate for a well-brought-up girl to express. She was also a very honest child, who could never bring herself to express sentiments which she did not feel or to praise what she disliked. This trait remained with her all her life, causing her considerable perplexity when in her role as Queen she knew that she ought to express sentiments which as a woman she could not feel. Throughout her life Victoria never learned to dissemble. Therefore, just because she lavished 'dear' and 'dearest' on the people on whom she was fond – and they were many – it is surely significant that, often as Lady Flora's name appears in her journal, it is never 'dear Lady Flora'.

Her steadiest affection, even devotion, was bestowed on her constant companion, Louise Lehzen. Originally she had come to England as governess to Victoria's half-sister Feodora, but had been the Princess's governess from 1824. She was the daughter of a German pastor, and to increase her social standing George IV created her a Hanoverian baroness in 1827. When by

24

1830 it was clear that Victoria would succeed her uncle, her mother decided that a governess of more exalted rank was desirable, and the Baroness was replaced as governess by the Duchess of Northumberland. This change did nothing to break the link between Lehzen and her young charge, as the Baroness then became Victoria's lady-in-waiting. This link between a teenage girl and an older woman, who is not only her constant companion but also is devoted to her, is, while it lasts, one of the closest ones that an adolescent can form. This is particularly true when, for any reason, the relationship between mother and daughter is of a more formal character. Lehzen was at once mentor, confidante, companion and idol, though in later life Victoria declared that though she adored the Baroness, she was nevertheless in some awe of her. In the journal she is described as 'my precious Lehzen', 'dearest best Lehzen' and, after the intolerable pressure to which she had been subjected by Sir John during her convalescence, it is surely significant that Victoria write in her journal '*dear good* Lehzen takes such care of me and is so unceasing in her attentions to me, that I shall never be able to repay her for all she has *borne* and done for me. She is the most affectionate, devoted, attached and *disinterested* friend I have, and I love her most *dearly*.' The underlining is surely significant. Even on the eve of her accession Victoria was to write that Lehzen was 'of course the greatest friend I have'. Though the Duchess of Kent devoted her life to what she conceived as the welfare of her daughter – insisting that even at night the Princess should sleep in her mother's room for fear of a sudden *coup* by the wicked Duke of Cumberland who, if Victoria died, would inherit the throne – and though in the pages of the journal Victoria expressed herself as a dutiful daughter should, there are far fewer 'dear Mamas' than 'dear Lehzens'.

Looking back over the years the Queen described her childhood as 'rather melancholy'. As far as companions of her own age were concerned it was certainly a lonely one. After her half-sister Feodora, who in any case was twelve years her senior, had married and gone to Germany, Victoria's only constant young playmate was Victoire Conroy, a companionship that after 1835 was increasingly poisoned by her detestation of Victoire's father. When after an absence of six years Feodora

Princess Feodora of Leiningen, Victoria's half-sister through the Duchess of Kent's first marriage. In 1828 she married Prince Ernest of Hohenlohe-Langenburg.

returned to England for a visit she was rapturously described by Victoria, now fourteen, as 'my DEAREST sister'. Victoria had a tremendous sense of family, which remained with her all her life. No doubt this was fostered by the prevailing assumption that one loved one's relations, but essentially it sprang from her own emotional and affectionate nature, which was starved of persons on whom to lavish her love. When she heard of the death of her aunt, Sophia Mensdorff-Pouilly, who was a sister of the Duchess of Kent, Victoria wrote 'My poor dear Aunt, I loved her *dearly* and feel the loss deeply. Time may weaken, but it can never, never efface the recollection of this loss.' Her grief might have sounded more convincing to modern readers if she had not also added, 'I should have been equally sad at losing her, had I *not* known her, because all Mama's relations are dear to me; but having seen her, having lived in the same house for more than a week . . . makes it more striking still, and makes me feel the weight of the loss we have experienced more'. As this visit had taken place two years before, the sixteen-year-old Victoria must, however unconsciously, have been dramatising her grief! Throughout her life she was prone to give a free rein to her emotions, which were never tepid.

Nevertheless there is something touching in the way in which Victoria welcomed the visits of her Coburg relations. Her entourage, except for the hated Sir John, and the older men whom she met briefly on social occasions, was almost completely feminine, so that as a growing teenager the young Princess had been starved of masculine companionship. Fortunately most of her visiting cousins were male, whom Victoria welcomed with delighted approval. When her Wurtemburg cousins, Ernest and Alexander, came to England in 1833 she described them as 'both *extremely tall*! Alexander is *very handsome* and Ernest has a *very kind expression*. They are both EXTREMELY *amiable*.' Even at the age of fourteen Victoria was very susceptible to manly beauty. When she heard in 1836 that her cousin Ferdinand, who had recently been married by proxy to Maria, the young Queen of Portugal, together with her uncle Ferdinand and her younger cousin Augustus, were to break their journey in England on their way to Portugal Victoria was once again delighted. Nor was she disappointed when they arrived. They were, she wrote, 'both dear and charming young men.

... I think Ferdinand handsomer than Augustus, his eyes are so beautiful and he has such a lively, clever expression.' They had arrived on 17 March and by April she was already lamenting 'Oh could I have some more such days, with that dear Uncle and dear Augustus, whom I love so much! I shall feel very lonely and unhappy when they leave us.' Later she wrote of Ferdinand that she loved him 'like the *dearest of brothers*'.

The pleasure which their visit gave Victoria soon paled when compared with that afforded her by the arrival of another uncle, Ernest, the reigning Duke of Saxe-Coburg, and his two sons, Ernest and Albert. Victoria was always interested in people's appearance, possibly because she was clever with her pencil and quick to catch a likeness. This was her first impression of her new cousins:

> Ernest is as tall as Ferdinand and Augustus; he has dark hair and fine dark eyes and eyebrows, but the nose and mouth are not good; he has a most kind, honest and intelligent expression in his countenance, and has a very good figure. Albert, who is just as tall as Ernest but stouter, is extremely handsome; his hair is about the same colour as mine; his eyes are large and blue, and he has a beautiful nose and a very sweet mouth with fine teeth; but the charm of his countenance is his expression, which is most delightful; *c'est à la fois* full of goodness and sweetness, and very clever and intelligent.

'*Albert ... is extremely handsome: his hair is about the same colour as mine*'

After one day of their company she wrote 'I like my Cousins extremely, they are so kind, so good and so merry.' The visit was a great success. Victoria thought that Albert was perhaps the more 'reflecting' of the brothers, but that they were both 'very, very merry and gay and happy' which she observed rather poignantly 'young people ought to be'. At this stage her affections seem to have been poured out impartially on both cousins. They were 'those *dearest*-beloved Cousins whom I *do* love so VERY VERY dearly; much more dearly than any other Cousins in the *world*'. When they left after a three-week visit Victoria embraced them both most warmly and cried 'bitterly, very bitterly'. But of all her relations throughout her girlhood Victoria was the most deeply attached to her Uncle Leopold, since 1830 the King of the Belgians.

No one could describe Victoria as a helpless clinging female, though in her early widowhood she endeavoured to portray

herself as such, but, combined with her intense obstinacy once her mind was made up, she had an innate need for some one person in her life, preferably male, on whom she could lean. In modern jargon, if she were to feel secure and happy she must have a 'father figure'. It was a matter of necessity for her to be able to pour out in unstinted measure her affection over whomsoever was cast to play this role in her life. Yet because she was both shrewd and honest, the recipient of her affection had also to be a person on whose judgment she relied and whose character she admired. She was fortunate that Fate provided her with five such men in her life, her uncle Leopold, Lord Melbourne, her husband, Disraeli and, in a rather different way, her Highland servant, John Brown. With all of them she enjoyed a very special relationship; each was associated with a different phase of her life, as a girl, as a young Queen, as a wife and as a widow. Probably it was inevitable that her uncle Leopold should be the man above all others to whom she looked up during her girlhood: the competition was negligible, the other constant male figure in her entourage being the hated Conroy. Until Leopold became King of the Belgians he continued to live at Claremont to which, even after 1830, he occasionally returned.

For the first years of Victoria's life her uncle represented both security and pleasure. As he was careful to remind his niece later it was he who, in the bitter winter of 1820, had journeyed to Sidmouth to comfort and sustain his widowed sister and her baby. It was he who had made it possible for them to remain in England at a time when there seemed little probability of his niece ever becoming Queen. Later, as he also reminded her, Claremont was 'where in younger days you were least plagued, and generally I saw you there in good spirits'. Though the same personal contacts were no longer possible once he had become King of the Belgians, Leopold never allowed Victoria to feel forgotten or neglected for long, though she did sometimes remonstrate that a letter was overdue. When her uncle wrote to her, he addressed her as 'My Dearest Love' and he never missed a birthday letter, in which affection was mingled with the good advice which nineteenth-century parents and relations thought it their duty to proffer to their young. By the time that Victoria was thirteen it was almost certain that she would succeed to the throne, and this inspired Leopold to write 'By the dispensation

OPPOSITE Princess Victoria with the Duchess of Kent in 1834; engraving by George Hayter.

of providence you are destined to fill a most eminent station, to fill it well must now become your study.' He then went on to reassure her that she 'will always find in your Uncle that faithful friend which he has proved to you from your earliest infancy, and whenever you feel yourself in want of support or advice, call on him with perfect confidence'. King Leopold was not only an affectionate uncle, he was also a consummate politician, well aware that bread now thrown upon the waters might return to him after many years in the shape of influence over the Queen of England.

Victoria was too young to realise this; her affection for her uncle was still unbounded and uncritical. When, after an absence of four years, Leopold and his second wife Louise, a daughter of Louis Philippe of France, were able to pay a visit to England, Victoria and her mother travelled down to Ramsgate to welcome them. In her journal that evening, 29 September 1835, his niece wrote joyfully 'What happiness it was for me to throw myself into the arms of that *dearest* of uncles who has always been to me like a father and whom I love so *very dearly*.' Next year, when he returned to Claremont, Victoria's journal once again brims over with admiration and love. 'He is *so* clever, *so* mild and *so* prudent; he alone can give me a good advice on *every* thing. His advice is perfect. He is indeed *"il mio secondo padre"* or rather *"solo padre"* for he is indeed like my own father, as I have none.' The bullying to which Sir John had subjected her since her uncle's last visit must have made Leopold's support doubly precious to his niece. By 1836 Leopold was preparing his niece for her future responsibilities. Victoria recorded that they talked over 'many important things'.

The days of her girlhood were nearly over. How far had they fitted her for the tasks that lay ahead? Most historians seem to agree that her education, though satisfactory enough for a girl destined for a private life, was intellectually mediocre for a future Queen of England. In fairness to her mother and the tutors chosen by her, it must be remembered that Victoria was not a natural academic. Later she made Lord Melbourne laugh by describing her tutor's horror at her 'false quantities', confessing that 'I thought I had benefitted but little by what I had learnt for that I could not construe any quotation.' Back came

'That dearest *of uncles who has always been to me like a father and whom I love so* very dearly'

30

the reassuring reply, 'Oh! yes you have. You know that there are such books, and such authors and what they are about.' Over the years Victoria had in fact managed to cover a fair amount of reading. Uncle Leopold, as always, was ready with advice, telling his niece that 'history is what I think the most important study for you. It will be difficult for you to learn humankind's ways and manners otherwise than from that important source of knowledge.' When he offered to supply a copy of Sully's *Memoirs* for this purpose Victoria wrote back accepting and telling her uncle that 'Reading History is one of my greatest delights' and that she was now reading Russell's *Modern Europe* and Clarendon's *History of the Rebellion* with her tutor the Rev. George Davys. In addition, she was amusing herself by making tables of the Kings and Queens, and she informed her uncle that she had just finished one 'of the English Sovereigns and their consorts, as, of course, the history of my own country is one of my first duties'. Six months later she wrote to say that she was reading Sully 'with great interest' and that she found in his *Memoirs* much that 'applies to the present times, and a great deal of good advice and reasoning in them', adding 'As you say, very truly, it is extremely necessary for me to follow the "events of the day", and to do so impartially.' Outside the hours of her regular studies she and Baroness Lehzen often read aloud to one another, a practice that she enjoyed later with her husband, and this reading aloud became a regular routine while Victoria's hair was being done in the morning. A typical entry in her journal reads 'Read out of Mde de Sévigné while my hair was doing to Lehzen.'

Some of the comments on what she read are revealing. Of Madame de Sévigné, Victoria wrote 'How truly elegant and natural her style is! It is so full of naïveté, cleverness and grace.' No one has ever described the Queen's own style as 'elegant', but the other adjectives might well be applied to the lively and often shrewd remarks contained in her own letters and in the journal. She might occasionally in later life have to consult Lord Melbourne on points of grammar and spelling, but nobody reading what Queen Victoria wrote was ever in two minds as to her meaning. Directness and simplicity were qualities which she valued in other people's books. *The Exposition of the Gospel of St Matthew* by the Bishop of Chester she thought 'a very fine book indeed', adding 'Just the sort of book I like: which is just plain and comprehensible and full of truth and good feeling.' Her liking for similar qualities in human beings appears again and again. She commended her singing master Lablache, as 'a most good humoured, pleasing, agreeable and honest man'. Her cousin Ferdinand talked 'so clearly and so sensibly', and on further acquaintance she wrote that she found him 'so sensible, so natural, so unaffected, and unsophisticated and so *truly* good'. These were the qualities which throughout her life she was to value highly. In addition to digesting what she read, Victoria was a reasonably good linguist. Lord Melbourne was of the opinion that 'as the world goes, she would, as any girl, have been considered accomplished, for she speaks German well and writes it; understands Italian, speaks French fluently, and writes it with great elegance'. Victoria herself was always painfully conscious of her limitations, particularly in the field of science. When, as a young Queen, she entertained Sir John Herschel to dinner, Victoria confessed that she 'did not profit' as much as she might have done from listening to the conversation between him and Lord Melbourne because 'I was stupid'. She was inclined to dislike and resent conversations from which she felt herself excluded, and as a consequence, when Queen, she was inclined to avoid the company of learned men.

Victoria found the acquisition of such accomplishments as were then deemed to be an essential part of any young lady's education a more congenial task. From an early age she was taught drawing, painting, singing, playing the piano and dancing, all of which, except possibly the piano, she enjoyed. She was good at sketching and made a practice of drawing from memory the various people she met, from gipsies to opera singers. Her singing lessons were a great source of pleasure. Her early master was John Sale, from St Margaret's, Westminster, but in 1835 she was promoted to study under Lablache. At her first lesson she was so nervous that she could hardly utter a sound, but he was a good teacher and she a good pupil. Nature had endowed Victoria with a clear and charming voice. Throughout her life people commented on the clear and bell-like tones with which she delivered her public speeches. During her girlhood, music, and in particular vocal music, was one of her greatest pleasures. Victoria adored the 'dear opera' and when she came to leave Kensington Palace for Buckingham Palace, she recalled nostalgically 'the delicious concerts' she had heard there. Her taste in music was for the tuneful and dramatic. She much preferred Rossini and Italian opera to Handel, whose *Messiah*, with the exception of one or two choruses and songs, she found 'heavy and tiresome'. Her favourite singer was Giulia Grisi, who was 'very young and pretty' and 'sang beautifully'.

Victoria was almost as devoted to the theatre, although after the Prince Consort's death she refused to attend public performances. In her early journals she describes at length the plays she has seen and the skill or otherwise with which the actors sustained their roles. In these appraisals there is the same stress on the qualities that Victoria most liked in people. For instance she was charmed with Charles Mathew who was 'so natural and amusing, and never vulgar but always the gentleman'. The simplicity of the life she led, combined with her mother's reluctance to take her daughter to Court, gave Victoria fewer opportunities to indulge her love of dancing. Her fourteenth birthday was therefore a red-letter day, because the King and Queen gave a ball for young people in her honour. She danced eight quadrilles and did not get home until half past twelve. She was, to use her highest term of praise, 'VERY much amused'. All her life, except in the bitter years of her widowhood, Victoria loved to dance, and in her graceful unselfconscious dignity looked her best on the dance floor. Her other physical girlhood recreation which gave her great pleasure, until her attack of typhoid, was riding her pony Rosa. As well as to her pony Victoria was devoted to her mother's King Charles Spaniel, Dash. When, as Queen, she moved to Buckingham Palace she was relieved to find that 'dear Dashy was quite happy' in his new garden. All her life Victoria was devoted to her dogs; in her eyes cruelty to animals was an unpardonable offence. When she lay dying she asked that her little Pomeranian, Turi, might be placed on her bed. Her mother, the Duchess of Kent, had taken great pains to bring her daughter up to be English in every way and in this at least she had served both Victoria and England well. The formative years, with their resentments and their pleasures, were nearly over for the girl who was so soon to become Queen of England.

WILLIAM IV DIED on 20 June 1837. The ill-feeling between the King and the Duchess of Kent persisted until his death. As late as 19 May, on the eve of the Princess's birthday, her uncle had sent her a personal letter offering her an independent income of £10,000 and her own establishment free of maternal control. This act, combined with the fact that the King's health was causing anxiety, determined Conroy and the Duchess to make a last effort to secure for Victoria's mother the Regency until her daughter became twenty-one. Every pressure that they could exert was brought to bear on her to agree 'voluntarily' to this arrangement, and every wile employed to convince influential people that Victoria was too young and too unfitted to rule. Attempts were even made to secure Leopold's support for this policy. Leopold, realising that a crisis was near, sent his *alter ego* and confidential adviser, Baron Stockmar, to London to hold a watching brief. It was the beginning of a long connection between him and the future Queen. As William IV's death became more certain, Leopold, not content with using Stockmar as his go-between, wrote constantly to his niece advising her on the pitfalls which might lie ahead and initiating her into the art of ruling, advice which his grateful niece told him she found most prudent and excellent. The days of brow-beating were nearly over for her.

How far was this girl of eighteen fitted to assume the responsibilities that were so soon to be hers? She certainly did not lack moral earnestness. Her birthday had always been a time for making good resolutions and on 24 May, almost on the eve of her accession, she recorded her resolve to be less trifling, not to let her attention wander from the task in hand, and in every way to fit herself for what one day she would become. The day before the King died, Victoria, writing to Leopold, expressed a certain quiet confidence, saying that though she did not feel completely equal to everything that lay ahead, yet she trusted that, aided by honesty, courage and good will, she would not be found wanting. Victoria could with justice claim all three qualities. The difficulties of the last two years had hardened and toughened her naturally gay and affectionate personality. As she wrote in her journal, though she was inexperienced in some ways she was not in others. Honest though Victoria was, and always would be, she had learned to keep her own counsel. Her

PREVIOUS PAGES Queen Victoria at her coronation, which took place on 28 June 1838. This incredibly romanticised portrayal was painted by Charles Robert Leslie.

RIGHT Victoria's uncle, Leopold, King of the Belgians, in 1855.

36

Queen Victoria holding
her first Privy Council,
painted by David Wilkie.
Wilkie purposely altered
the Queen's robe from
black to white to
emphasise the innocence of
the young Queen at her
first public appearance.
Melbourne is shown
holding the pen, with
Palmerston on his left and
Russell on his right.
Wellington stands before
the pillar with Peel on
his left, and the Dukes of
Cumberland and Sussex
seated at the table.

courage and obstinacy had combined to resist pressures and
attempts to override her will. There was a debit side: caught in
a web from which she had been unable to escape, Victoria had
come to resent those persons, even her own mother, who had
tried to dominate her. Victoria's stifled longing for independence can be observed from the ways in which she used her new
freedom. Again and again in the days following her accession
the fact that she rejoiced at last to be standing on her own feet is
underlined by the frequent use of the word 'alone' in her journal, whether she was recording having seen her ministers for the
first time, or enjoying at last the privacy of a bedroom to herself. Later it gave her great pleasure to be able to entertain her
beloved Uncle Leopold and his wife under her own roof. From
the beginning the young Queen threw herself into her new life
with zest; though it involved hard work, she delighted in discussing business with her ministers. Far from her new duties
proving a burden, she told her uncle that she was sleeping well
and found time to go driving in the country every evening.

38

Victoria was informed of her uncle's death by the Archbishop of Canterbury and Lord Conyngham. She was aroused from her sleep and received them in a hastily-donned dressing-gown. Her dignity and self-possession, in spite of her small stature – Victoria was only five foot two inches – surprised and delighted her ministers and her Privy Council. From the very beginning she assumed control and took the reins firmly in her own small hands. To any one who had known what had been happening behind the scenes at Kensington Palace this self-control might have seemed less surprising. The machinations of Sir John and her mother must have underlined the desirability of that power for which they had struggled, while her own sufferings in defending her right to retain it could not but make it still more precious in her eyes. Moreover, Victoria would have been less than human if, during those two painful years, she had not looked forward to the time when she would be Queen and in her mind pictured herself playing that role. Little as she had been at Court, kingship could have held no mystery in her eyes. Her grandfather and two of her uncles had been kings of England, her beloved Uncle Leopold was a king, and most of her relations ruled over independent, though sometimes small, principalities in Europe. Anyone as shrewd as Victoria cannot have supposed that she would cut a less satisfactory figure than her uncle William IV. Sir Sidney Lee's description of her predecessors as 'an imbecile, a profligate and a buffoon' is something less than fair, nevertheless the standard of kingship that they had set could not be described as daunting to a courageous, honest young woman of eighteen. Moreover, though inexperienced in some ways, she had the benefit of the advice of one of her uncles, the cleverest politician of his day, who in his letters stressed to her the importance of establishing a regular routine for both handling State papers and seeing her ministers. He warned her against making hasty decisions, pointing out that it was often extremely difficult to retreat from a decision once made. In addition to the remote control that Leopold was so anxious to exercise, Victoria knew that she could always turn to the invaluable Stockmar if she felt the need for a more immediate confidant.

Both were soon to be overshadowed by her Prime Minister, Lord Melbourne. Occasionally two people find themselves the ideal complement of one another, and their needs and temperaments dovetail into one another as neatly as pieces in a jigsaw. So, until her marriage, it was to be with Victoria and Lord Melbourne. On her accession he was a disillusioned man of fifty-eight, with a tragic personal history behind him. His wife, Lady Caroline Lamb, had been mentally unbalanced; all Society had gossiped about her wild attachment to Lord Byron. Until her death in 1826, William Lamb, as Melbourne then was, had shown her patience and tenderness that was above all praise. Later his only son by that unfortunate marriage, an epileptic, also died. Melbourne's success in politics was no compensation for the torment of his private life. He was in politics because as a Whig peer it was almost inevitable that he should be. When Lord Althorp succeeded his father and withdrew from active politics, Melbourne, becoming Prime Minister almost by default, voted it 'a damned bore' and wondered whether to accept. His politics were those of the orthodox Whigs, who should not be confused with the Radicals or with the future Liberals, merely because they had collaborated with them to pass the Reform Act of 1832. The genuine Whig outlook was aristocratic not reforming. Melbourne's first instinct was to leave things alone. He confessed frankly that he did not like the middle classes, considering that they were all affectation, conceit, pretence and concealment. Disillusioned and unambitious, he was very much a man of the world, well-informed, witty, endowed with great charm of manner, a beautiful speaking voice and an uninhibited laugh. Victoria found him a merry and stimulating conversationalist. Again and again in her journal she reported his funny and extravagant remarks and opinions, many of which went to form her own ways of thinking until later her husband's views came to dominate hers. Melbourne was relaxed, tolerant of the ways of Society, and had a fund of stories and gossip about both her own family and the polite world which helped to fill in the gaps left by her secluded girlhood.

Their roles were reciprocal, for underneath Melbourne's charm, affability and bonhomie a well of frustrated affection had accumulated. If his life were not to be emotionally barren, he desperately needed someone on whom to lavish the stored-up affection of the years, someone to whom he was a necessity.

Now Fate, with unexpected generosity, had imposed on him the demanding task of training a young and charming girl to be a queen. Almost immediately he won her liking and regard. After her first conversation with him as Prime Minister Victoria bestowed on him the accolade of her favourite adjectives; he was straightforward, honest, clever and a good man. In the evening they had what the Queen described as a very comfortable as well as important talk, so that she already felt more and more confidence in him. Victoria admired his looks and found his manner kind. This was such a pleasant change from the last years of her girlhood at Kensington Palace. By mid-July she was calling Melbourne her friend, but he was

William Lamb, 2nd Viscount Melbourne: painted by J. Partridge in 1844. Melbourne was to provide the support and friendship vital to Victoria in the opening years of her reign.

41

One of Victoria's first public engagements as Queen was to ride to the Guildhall to dine with the Lord Mayor and the City Corporation. This engraving shows the Queen's procession passing through Trafalgar Square, with the National Gallery and St Martin's-in-the-Fields in the background, on 9 November 1837.

rapidly becoming more than that. Victoria had found a new 'father figure' and Melbourne a substitute daughter. In the weeks to come he and Lehzen, whom he had the good sense not to antagonise, sustained the young Queen through all the ceremonies and ordeals which a new reign inevitably entailed. Mama was very firmly pushed into the background, being merely a lay figure on State occasions. Meanwhile Victoria was winning golden opinions with her youthful composure and dignity, whether proroguing Parliament, holding a chapter of the Garter (which, incidentally, she loved to wear on all occasions) or being entertained by the Lord Mayor. Wherever she appeared, she was greeted by loyal and enthusiastic crowds promising a new *rapprochement* between the Queen and her people. This reached its climax on the day of her coronation, which took place on 28 June 1838, just over a month after her nineteenth birthday. All London was *en fête* with the guns in the Park thundering out their salute at four o'clock in the morning. After this there was no sleep for anyone, not even the Queen.

When the great day came, Victoria was quite calm. At ten o'clock, having eaten a little breakfast before she dressed, and a little more afterwards, she entered the State Coach. The procession reached the Abbey a little after 11.30. The day was fine (it usually was for Victoria so that 'the Queen's weather' became proverbial) and all along the route the procession was

42

Figurine in Staffordshire pottery showing the Queen in her crown and robes.

greeted with thunderous cheers. Victoria was clearly delighted with her reception. She wrote with emotion of her loyal subjects, declaring 'I really cannot say *how* proud I feel to be the Queen of *such* a *Nation*.' Once the actual ceremony began, however, many of the participants did not seem to know what they should be doing. The aged Archbishop of Canterbury mistimed the delivery of the orb and crushed the Coronation ring onto the wrong finger, so that it proved very painful to take off. To add a touch of the ridiculous, eighty-two-year-old Lord Rolle, while tottering up the steps to kiss the Queen's hand, overbalanced and fell down again, so that to prevent a repetition of the accident Victoria went to the head of the steps, a spontaneous and kindly gesture that was characteristic of her warm heart. Through the long ceremonies the Queen was sustained by the presence of Melbourne, who reassured her with a fatherly look, and of Lehzen, with whom Victoria exchanged a smile as she sat on the throne. When she returned to the Palace, she declared that she was not really tired, though later at dinner, when she, Melbourne and the royal party were holding a post mortem on the day's events she did confess that her feet were a little tired. She had, however, 'the gratifying feeling that her duty had been done' when Lord Melbourne, with tears in his eyes, told her how beautifully she had acquitted herself. She would, she confided to her journal, always 'remember this day as the *proudest* of my life'. Above all, the young Queen was moved by the enthusiasm and affection of the vast crowds who packed every vantage place on the route. Londoners proverbially enjoyed a ceremony, whether it was a royal procession or, in earlier days, a mass hanging at Tyburn. Both made a welcome break in lives that were, for most, drab and hard. Nevertheless the enthusiasm with which Victoria's coronation was greeted owed at least something to the good will of the Londoners for their young and charming Queen, after a long succession of most uninspiring monarchs.

The first years of Victoria's reign formed one of the happiest, or at least the most carefree periods of her life, though later she was to disparage their artificial gaiety when compared with the deep happiness she was to know in her life with Albert. At the time, however, life seemed very pleasant indeed. After the unhappiness of the last years it was wonderful to be the person around whom everything and everybody appeared to revolve. Victoria was now able to take up riding again, and was enthusiastic about her new mounts. When, towards the end of August, the Court went to Windsor, Victoria began to ride regularly and her pleasure was undoubtedly enhanced because Lord Melbourne was so often one of the party. When it became time to return to London Victoria was sad to go. It had been, she said, 'the pleasantest summer I EVER passed in my *life*'. London, too, had its pleasures. Victoria resumed her singing lessons with her old teacher Lablache and was also able to indulge her love of dancing. In the May of 1838 the Queen gave her first State ball and doubtless no guest enjoyed it more than she did. She danced every dance except the waltzes; though waltzes had been danced for some little time, they were still looked upon slightly askance by the prudish, and Victoria was of the opinion, endorsed by Melbourne, that to circle the floor in a young man's arms, was rather over-familiar behaviour for a young woman in her position. Later, to waltz with Albert was one of her pleasures. In spite of her self-denying ordinance she declared that it was a lovely ball and that she had felt so merry and gay. On her birthday the Queen gave another splendid ball, which went on until dawn, so that she was not, she recorded gleefully, in bed until it was broad daylight! All in all, it was the happiest birthday that she had spent for years.

Much as Victoria enjoyed her riding and her dancing, she also derived much simple pleasure from evenings spent at Windsor, or Buckingham Palace with her immediate household and a few chosen guests, of whom, at least three or four times a week, Melbourne was one. The Queen usually sat on the sofa, which she shared with a favoured companion; Lord Melbourne sat on a chair near to her while the rest of the company gathered round the table. Sometimes the whole party played merry games, but more often the Queen and Lord Melbourne dominated the conversation, she asking his views on all manner of subjects, and he delivering them on any topic from 'queasy stomachs' in children – based on the fact that as a child he had been made to eat boiled mutton and rice pudding – to the education of the working class. Sometimes they looked at illustrated books, such as Lodge's *Portraits*, which he enlivened by anecdotes concerning the originals, to Victoria's

great delight. Many were the evenings spent in this atmosphere of relaxed domesticity. It was not long before the Queen began to expect Lord M., as she called him in her journal, to spend all his time with her and to grudge him to his older friends, even outside the hours that were necessarily devoted to business. Again and again she writes of him as being 'fatherly' and of his kindness in explaining difficult matters to her much as if she had been in fact his child. Both in her work and in her play her Prime Minister had become the most important person in Victoria's life.

The idealistic quality of the first years of her reign was not to continue. By the end of 1838 the storm clouds that were to darken the sunshine of her first year were gathering. Much of the subsequent trouble the Queen brought upon herself was because she had allowed resentment against Sir John Conroy and her mother to affect her judgment. Towards Queen Adelaide, Victoria displayed a compassionate tact, continuing to address her as Queen and making her always welcome at Court, but her own mother was pointedly excluded from her private life, although for form's sake mother and daughter appeared together in public. In private the Duchess was isolated

Victoria riding with Melbourne at Windsor: painting by Sir Francis Grant.

in her own quarters, unable even to visit her daughter's apartments without permission. A part of the trouble, as always, was Sir John. The Duchess had been anxious that the Queen should show him some mark of favour, instead Victoria had promptly excluded him from the royal household. She could not, however, prevent him from continuing to be her mother's comptroller and the Duchess refused to part with the man whom she continued to regard as an old and loyal friend. It was not until the middle of 1839 that the Duke of Wellington finally persuaded him to leave, and by then the mischief had been done. Meanwhile Lehzen, taking her revenge for the years in which Conroy had made her life a misery because of her partisanship of Victoria, was fanning the fires of the royal resentment. The ties that had bound the Queen to the Baroness had remained as firm as ever; indeed so bitter were Victoria's feelings towards her real mother that perversely she began to substitute the Baroness for the Duchess, addressing her as 'dearest mother Lehzen'. With an adoring adopted 'father', who saw the situation through her eyes and a jealously possessive spinster cast to play the role of 'mother', it is hardly surprising that confronted with the temptation of damaging the reputation of one of the Duchess of Kent's most faithful friends, Victoria found herself the victim of her own poisoned emotions. The temptation to retaliate came at a time when Victoria was nervously exhausted and therefore particularly vulnerable. After the first heady delights of being Queen she was suffering from a very natural reaction: she was, after all, barely twenty. Moreover, Lord Melbourne had become almost an obsession with her; she was jealous when he spent any time with his old friend Lady Holland, and irritable whenever she thought she was not the centre of his attention. Moreover, there was a nagging worry as to the political situation; Melbourne's ministry was weak and under increasing pressure from the Tory leader, Sir Robert Peel. Suddenly, activities which had seemed so exciting and so satisfying ceased to satisfy. Victoria had run into one of those phases of nervous irritability in which her emotions not only took control but also drove her into harbouring suspicions for which there was little justification. The result was disastrous for the young Queen's reputation.

The central figure in the tragedy was Lady Flora Hastings,

who since 1832 had been a member of the Duchess of Kent's household and thus an omnipresent figure from the resented past. Neither Victoria nor Lehzen liked her because, apart from any clash of temperament, she had been a member of the Conroy clique, but after the Queen's accession she still retained her position as lady-in-waiting to the Duchess. When Lady Flora returned to her duties at the Palace after spending Christmas with her family in Scotland she shared a post-chaise with Sir John on the journey back to London. On her arrival, Lady Flora, feeling unwell, consulted Sir James Clark, who since 1835 had been the Duchess's physician. He did not take her illness very seriously, merely prescribing rhubarb and ipecacuanha pills. Whatever the trouble was, it did not prevent Lady Flora from dining at the Palace that day. Two days later Victoria and Lehzen thought that they detected an interesting change in Lady Flora's figure and, because nothing was too bad to attribute to either her or Sir John, they began to speculate as to whether she were pregnant. The mystery has never been completely solved of how Sir James Clark came to share their suspicions; rumours then began to circulate among the Queen's ladies. Instead of approaching either Lady Flora herself, or the Duchess of Kent, Lady Tavistock, the senior of the ladies-of-the-bedchamber, raised the matter with Melbourne. He, true to character, advised waiting. He did not, however, dismiss the whole idea as nonsense, possibly swayed partly by the vehemence of Victoria's feelings and partly because he was not altogether sorry to see the name of Hastings (the family were staunch Tories) smirched by scandal. Moreover Melbourne belonged to a generation that would not have been unduly shocked or surprised if Lady Flora had indeed been pregnant. Indeed, in view of Sir James's doubts he may well have believed this to be the case. It was not until February, when Lady Portman came into waiting and decided that the matter could not be allowed to drift, that Lady Flora was confronted with the ugly rumour and the Duchess was also told.

With courage and dignity Lady Flora then agreed to be examined by Sir James and his colleague Sir George Clarke. At a time when a woman's physical functions were obscured by a veil of sensibility and sentimentality, to submit to such an examination was a brave act, and when it was revealed that

Lady Flora Hastings, the unfortunate lady-in-waiting to the Duchess of Kent, from an engraving by Findon. Blame for her hounding and subsequent death was laid by general opinion at Victoria's door, and the monarchy suffered considerable unpopularity as a result.

47

Lady Flora was a virgin, this ought to have terminated the scandal. The Queen was personally upset by the false position in which she had placed both herself and Lady Flora by neither scotching the rumours nor warning her mother about them, and did what she could to undo the harm by sending expressions of regret and a request to see Lady Flora. But it was not until a week later that the maligned woman, shattered by both ill health and her ordeal, felt strong enough to see the Queen. By then the situation was again worsening, and gossip began to leak through to the Press. Also the doctors who had made the examination seem to have been trying to cover themselves by hinting that, even when a woman was technically a virgin, pregnancies had been known to occur. People conscious of having wronged someone are inclined to welcome any explanation which can be put forward to imply that the person so wronged was in fact substantially guilty, or at least that there was reason to believe this to be so. Certainly both the Queen and Melbourne seem to have snatched at the straws of the doctors' doubts and continued to convince themselves that Lady Flora was indeed pregnant. Meanwhile both the Duchess and the Hastings family were asking how the rumour had arisen in the first case. If the culprit was Sir James Clark, who

Cartoon of January 1838, showing John Bull supporting a seesaw, on the left hand of which sits Wellington, the Tory leader, while Melbourne, leader of the Whigs, rides high at the other end. The young Queen stands in the centre, but plainly shows her preference for the Whigs and Melbourne.

48

was also the Queen's physician, why had she not dismissed him from her service as the Duchess had immediately done? Instead, with her usual loyalty to her friends, Victoria continued to support him. By so doing she raised yet another of those fascinating questions of history: namely, if Sir James had not still been her chief medical adviser in 1861, would more effective treatment for typhoid have been applied earlier to the Prince Consort, and if so, would it have made any difference? Even the immediate effects of the Queen's obstinacy were calamitous. A letter which Lady Flora had written to her uncle, giving him the details of the whole miserable story, was published in *The Examiner*. The publicity which Melbourne had dreaded had arrived. The Queen's popularity plummeted, and she could no longer bring herself to speak to Lady Flora.

Meanwhile political troubles were looming. In 1839 Britain, like her Queen, was going through a bad phase. Trade had been depressed since 1837 bringing with it unemployment, especially in the urban areas where the attempts to introduce and enforce the new Poor Law Amendment Act of 1834 had led to rioting. Working-class discontent gave rise to a new movement of protest, known as Chartism because the demands were contained in the six points of the People's Charter. These were constitutional in form, but economic in motivation, and when backed by rallies and conventions they aroused all those latent fears of social revolution which had terrified the propertied classes since the French Revolution. In addition, the middle-class industrialists were organising the powerful Anti-Corn Law League to campaign for the abolition of the Corn Laws, which they argued hindered the expansion of trade and industry by keeping the price of bread artificially high and discouraging foreign imports. As this programme was commonly regarded as a threat to the agricultural interest, so strongly represented in Parliament, this too was a symptom of new pressures on the social and economic fabric of the kingdom. Even within the ministry, the Radical section, which Melbourne and therefore the Queen disliked, was pressing for further measures of reform, while Peel was waiting quietly in the wings for the ministry to fall through its own weakness. The day on which Victoria would lose her often sorely-tried father figure was drawing horribly close. That dread, combined with the Lady

Landseer's painting
of *Windsor Castle in
modern times*, showing
Victoria and Albert
with their eldest daughter,
the Princess Royal, in
the early 1840s. Albert is
portrayed sitting with his
dogs and the game
which he has shot, while
his demure wife stands
admiring him.
The Queen described
this picture as 'very
cheerful and pleasing'.

Flora affair, must have made the Queen feel 'How all occasions do inform against me', although when the ministry was actually defeated in May the combination of obstinacy and personal feeling, which had been her undoing in the Hastings affair, enabled her for a time, unlike Canute, to keep back the Tory tide.

There is every indication that by then Victoria was feeling shaken, even desperate. The miserable business of Lady Flora was still hanging over her; Sir John remained her mother's comptroller, and the Queen was beginning to develop what might almost be described as a persecution mania against both the Duchess and Sir John. In her private conversations with Melbourne she seemed incapable of getting away from this distressing topic. By now her one desire was to contrive her mother's departure from the Palace, yet convention decreed that, even though she was a Queen, as a young unmarried woman she could not openly shake off her maternal protection. The only alternative was one which Victoria viewed at this time with much misgiving, namely marriage. Clearly she was a very perplexed and unhappy young woman and to lose the support of her 'excellent Melbourne' was something that she could not bring herself to contemplate. Yet, because he had drilled her in her duties as a constitutional monarch they both realised that if he were no longer her Prime Minister the old routine of daily letters and talks, cosy dinner parties enlivened by his fund of information and his funny remarks, indeed everything that made her life bearable at this difficult time, must come to an end. After his defeat in the House, Lord Melbourne was forced to tell her that he could neither come to dinner that night nor even call afterwards, and that while negotiations for a new ministry were going on he must not see the Queen at all. Both the elderly politician and the young woman were on the brink of tears throughout the painful conversation in which he finally told her that he must resign. Victoria recorded her 'dreadful state of grief', while Melbourne told her that nothing had ever given him more pain than having to tell her that he must resign. When he gave her his hand she could hardly let it go and his look of mingled pity and affection made her almost choke with tears so that she could hardly speak. What came to be known as 'the Bedchamber Question' must be seen against this background of personal grief.

Victoria intended to do her duty as a constitutional monarch, as she saw that duty to be. She was perhaps unfortunate in that the conception of her role was in a state of flux, though this also gave her more room for manœuvre than would be permitted a twentieth-century sovereign. George III had certainly considered himself to be a constitutional king in that he had no intention of overriding either the Law or the will of Parliament legally expressed. Nevertheless, he regarded ministers as his servants and felt that he had a right to expect Parliament not to attack them for purely party political motives. Indeed, as late as his accession in 1760, it was still generally accepted that the choice of ministers rested with the King, though this choice had to be acceptable also to the majority of the Commons. The closing years of George III's reign had seen this convention substantially eroded; William IV had been the last sovereign to assert his right to choose his own ministers in the hope that Parliament would ratify his choice, by giving his support to Peel and Wellington when, in the November of 1834, he had asked them to form a ministry to replace the Whigs. In the general election which followed in December, Peel failed, in spite of the support of the Crown, to gain an overall majority and though Peel held on briefly in the February of 1835 a combination of Whigs, Radicals and Irish Members forced him to resign in favour of Lord Melbourne. Henceforth it was clear that the Crown could no longer expect the Commons to support ministers merely because they had the royal confidence. Melbourne had educated Victoria to accept this as a fact of political life and she realised that, as Queen, she must ask a set of men whom she confessed to dislike to form a ministry. So far the constitutional position was clear and to this extent the Queen was prepared to do her duty, though she hoped that the Duke of Wellington and not Sir Robert Peel, to whom she had taken a great dislike, might be her new Prime Minister.

What was constitutionally less clear was to what extent the change of ministry must be reflected in the changes in the royal household. Unfortunately this had been composed solely of Whigs. Victoria herself was a passionate Whig and made no pretence of being anything else. The Whigs were her friends, the Tories her enemies. Constitutional practice had not yet hardened to the extent that it imposed a strict neutrality on the

Sir Robert Peel, leader of the Tory party by 1839. He was unable to form a government in that year due to the Queen's obstinacy over the Bedchamber Question. Portrait by J. Linell, painted in 1838.

monarch, but Sir Robert could hardly view with equanimity a Court that was peopled exclusively by his political enemies. The composition of the household therefore came to seem an important political question. Melbourne was anxious to soften the blow of his having to leave her, realising that if at the same time Victoria were to be faced with the loss of the familiar persons who had surrounded her since her accession, she would be put under an additional strain when she was already finding her situation almost more than she could bear. He therefore

54

made what proved to be a most dangerous suggestion. This was that in her negotiations with Peel she had better express the hope that none of her household, except those members who were actively engaged in politics, would be removed. This in effect meant that none of her ladies – even if their husbands were known opponents of the Tories – could be replaced by Tories. To the Queen this seemed a reasonable stipulation. She was prepared to change her ministers in accordance with the will of the Commons and she would even replace the gentlemen of her household who were active politicians and Members of Parliament, but she was not prepared to give up her ladies, whose relationship with her, she argued, was personal not political.

It was upon this rock that the negotiations with Peel broke down. Though it took the form of a constitutional crisis, the tussle was in reality a clash of personalities. Melbourne had described Peel as a stiff, cold man. He was certainly not the type to establish easy relations with an impulsive, emotional and harrassed young woman. In his political career he very rarely allowed either his own personal interests or his likes and dislikes to sway his actions when he thought that the interests of the country were involved, and he did not find it easy to accept the fact that other people were not capable of the same degree of detachment. Peel was respected by many, but the number who liked and appreciated him were few. In later years one of these was to be Prince Albert – and surprisingly the Queen herself came to like him. Moreover, Peel was suffering from the further disadvantage of filling a high political position traditionally reserved for the wellborn. True, his father, also Sir Robert Peel, had been created a baronet, but the Peel fortune had been made in cotton. It is true also that Lord Melbourne professed ignorance of his own grandfather, which Victoria thought very fine in him, but about Peel there still hung the aura of being not 'quite a gentleman', – Victoria likened him to a dancing master – while 'dear Lord Melbourne' was a peer. Sir Robert therefore faced the obstinate young woman at a considerable disadvantage.

At first the negotiations, opened by the old Duke of Wellington, seemed to be going uneventfully, although the Queen wrote to Melbourne that she had the impression that Peel was

'I said I could not give up any of my Ladies, and never had imagined such a thing'

neither happy nor sanguine. Though Victoria prided herself on having shown no agitation, she can hardly have displayed the warmth necessary to put a man like Peel at his ease, aware as he was of the Queen's preference for Melbourne. In subsequent interviews all went smoothly until Sir Robert raised the question of her ladies. Indignantly the Queen replied that she refused to give up any of them. Did she mean them all, the Mistress of the Robes and the ladies of the Bedchamber? 'All' was the uncompromising reply. The result was a genuine *impasse*. Victoria was determined not to lose her ladies and considered it outrageous that she should be asked to do so. Sir Robert argued that he must have some proof of her confidence in her new ministers and that many of the ladies in question were the wives of his political opponents. Victoria countered this argument by declaring that she never talked politics with her ladies, which was probably technically true. One root of the difficulty was that neither the Queen nor Peel could quote a firm precedent; Victoria was the first Queen regnant since Anne, when the constitutional position of the monarchy had been very different. Since then the Queen's household had been merely that of a consort.

After the interview Victoria informed Melbourne that she had never seen so frightened a man! Clearly she thought that she was getting the best of the battle, for she warned Melbourne to be prepared for what might happen in the next few hours. Meanwhile the Duke of Wellington did his best to administer a lecture on the constitutional issues to the indignant Queen, pointing out that it was quite irrelevant whether she talked politics to her ladies or not, for the issue was a matter of principle. In spite of anything that either the Duke or Peel could say, Victoria was convinced that she was only defending her rights and that it would be absurd if Peel broke off negotiations because she refused to give up her ladies.

This determined young woman had got both Lord Melbourne and Sir Robert Peel where she wanted them. She informed Peel that she could not agree to a course of action that was both contrary to usage and repugnant to her feelings, and then communicated to Melbourne what she had said. Peel refused to accept office on these terms, and shook Melbourne somewhat when in his letter declining to do so, the Prime

Minister designate made it clear that he had asked the Queen to make only *some* changes in her ladies whereas the Queen had consistently implied that she was being faced with a demand that she should replace them *all*. When Melbourne raised this discrepancy, Victoria argued with the kind of logic which is sometimes described as feminine that there was no difference between 'some' and 'all'. Even so, Lord Melbourne felt that he must put the entire situation to his Cabinet before he was able to continue. Sentiment and the spectacle of a forlorn young Queen fighting for her ladies, won her the Cabinet's support, and Sir Robert and the Tories retired defeated. Victoria kept her 'father figure' for another two years. She had fought her campaign with tenacity and skill. Had she genuinely believed that Peel had intended to make a clean sweep of her household? She certainly told Melbourne that Peel was such a cold, odd man that she was never sure that she understood his meaning, so there may have been some failure in communication. Or had she in fact persuaded herself that there was no essential difference between 'some' and 'all'? Whatever the case, it was no mean achievement, and indicative of her toughness, loyalty and sheer cleverness when fighting for a cause in which she believed.

The end of the Lady Flora affair was less happy. Ugly rumours continued to circulate. At Ascot, where Victoria, accompanied by Melbourne, rode up the course, two Tory ladies hissed at her from the grandstand. On another occasion there were shouts of 'Mrs Melbourne' from the crowd. By the end of June it was clear that, whatever the cause, Lady Flora was dying. On 27 June the Queen, in a belated gesture of sympathy, nerved herself to visit the doomed woman, who died on 5 July. Before she died, she had insisted that a *post mortem* should be performed to clear her name, and this revealed the fact that she had died of a tumour on the liver. This had been the unknown cause of the suspicious swelling. Her body was taken by ship to her family home in Scotland, where the funeral was turned into almost a mute anti-Victoria protest. In London, when the Queen sent a carriage to join the cortège which accompanied the body on the first stage of its journey to the wharf, the carriage had a few stones hurled at it. Gone was the popularity of the gay young Queen, who now looked set to become as unloved a figure as her two uncles had been before her.

Take this fellow He'll suit us best.

3 Courtship and Marriage 1839-40

By 1839 VICTORIA was faced with yet another problem, the question of her future marriage. The heir to the throne was her unpopular uncle, the Duke of Cumberland who, because women were barred by Hanoverian law from the throne, had succeeded his brother William IV as King of Hanover, and thus broken the link between the two countries which dated from the accession of George I. Not only was her uncle unpopular, but his son was blind. There were therefore very sound reasons why, unless Britain and Hanover were to be reunited under a king unacceptable to the British people, Victoria should marry and produce an heir. The question was bound to arise in her many conversations with Melbourne, and in July the Queen told him that the whole subject was odious to her and that, if possible, she would prefer never to marry at all, a pronouncement which he greeted with some doubt. He did however assure her that, though he had expected some public anxiety on the matter, there appeared to be none. He was able therefore to agree with her to the extent that, until some impatience was shown, there was no need to make any decisions at the moment. Victoria could certainly afford to wait a year or two. Her reluctance may appear somewhat surprising: since the visit of her Coburg cousins, Albert and Ernest, in 1836 Victoria had apparently accepted the fact that her uncle Leopold was planning a marriage between her and the younger of the two cousins, Albert, and she had certainly shown no aversion to the project then. After their visit she had written to her uncle to thank him for the prospect of 'great happiness' which she foresaw in the person of 'dear Albert', whom she declared possessed every quality that could make her happy. She then listed them, writing 'He is so sensible, so kind, and so good, and so amiable too. He has besides, the most pleasing and delightful exterior and appearance you can possibly see.'

Since that first meeting there had been no further personal contact between the two young people; on her accession, Albert had sent his cousin merely a correct and formal little note of congratulation. From her later correspondence with her uncle, it is clear that as late as April 1838 Victoria still regarded Albert as her future husband, but a note of impersonality had crept into their relationship. Leopold was busily grooming the young Prince to be the husband of the Queen of England, and

60

Prince Albert of
Saxe-Coburg-Gotha:
portrait by Winterhalter.

61

Winterhalter's portrait of
Victoria, Albert
and five of their children,
painted in 1846.
The children are left to
right, Alfred, the
Prince of Wales, Alice,
Helena and Vicky.

62

was consulting Victoria as to the best method of directing his education to fit him for this position. In so doing, Leopold assured his niece that he was most anxious to see Albert grow into a very good and distinguished young man, and that he personally would spare no pains to achieve this goal. After a correspondence, distinctly unemotional on Victoria's side, it was decided that a course of foreign travel, with Stockmar acting as bear-leader, would be the best plan. Albert himself does not seem to have been too happy about his future prospects, writing to his much-loved tutor, 'I am to go into society, learn the ways of the world and vitiate my culture with fashionable accomplishments', adding the slightly bitter comment 'the last of which would appear to be an extraordinary good testimonial in Victoria's eyes'. However, he was resigned to go through with it, hoping only that his personal integrity might not suffer in the process. At somewhat infrequent intervals Stockmar made a report to Victoria, for instance telling her that in Rome Albert had made such thorough use of his time that he had left no major sight unseen. They even visited the Vatican, and later Albert gave a lively and amusing account of a papal audience, which shows the Prince's mirthful appreciation of the ridiculous as he watched a cleric attempting to kiss the papal foot. Neither Leopold nor Victoria seem to have felt any impropriety in so directing Albert's life, but any young man might be forgiven for finding his future wife playing so important a part in moulding his education galling to his pride. It was well indeed that Albert was sensible, good and kind. They were all virtues which he was to need in the future.

When Victoria finally nerved herself to discuss the question of her marriage, her attitude was still one of temporising. She started by asking Melbourne if he knew that King Leopold's great wish was that she should marry her cousin Albert, and said that she had told her uncle she could decide nothing until she had met Albert again. Melbourne's attitude was equally luke-warm. He was inclined to stress the unpopularity of the Coburgs who, he said, were not liked abroad. The Queen, whose latent obstinacy was always aroused by any hint of opposition, then asked Melbourne if there was anyone else equally suitable. When they went through the list of possibles, they decided there was not. Once again Victoria reiterated that

'I am to go into society, learn the ways of the world and vitiate my culture with fashionable accomplishments'

her feelings were against matrimony either then or later, but that from all she had heard about him, Albert would be 'just the person'. Melbourne was inclined to disagree. He told the Queen that he did not like the idea of her marrying a cousin, and reminded her that foreigners were not popular in England. At the same time he was forced to agree that to marry a subject could lead to all kinds of jealousies and difficulties. Finally they agreed that it was not necessary to do anything definite for another three or four years. Leopold was not content to accept this policy of drift and by July 1838 was pressing his niece to give her consent to a visit from Ernest and Albert in the autumn. Once again Victoria declared that she had very little desire to see Albert. It is interesting to speculate about her reasons for this reluctance.

Her reaction was in many ways a natural one. It marks the gulf that divided the schoolroom miss, who had only recently passed her seventeenth birthday, from the twenty-year-old young woman, who for two years had been 'queening it' in the drawing rooms and ball-rooms of London. Until her accession, Victoria had been kept on the tightest of maternal reins and, though much had gone awry in the past year, independence was still sweet to her. To marry was to relinquish at least some of it. The position of a wife at this period was one of subordination: She was her husband's chattel: he could legally beat her – within limits – lock her up, deny her access to her children; all her property, unless tied up in a settlement before marriage, belonged to her husband, even her earnings after marriage were legally his. Victoria knew, of course, that there was no danger of any of these things happening to her personally, but it was difficult for her to shake off the assumptions and conventions of the society of which she was a member. Moreover, Victoria was sufficiently intelligent, as well as conventionally-minded, to realise that with marriage some part of her new and delightful independence must be sacrificed. Much later, in 1858, when writing to her own newly-married eldest daughter, she spoke of 'the yoke of a married woman', though she also by then could write of 'the unbounded happiness if one has a husband one worships. It is a foretaste of heaven'. But in 1839 she had not learned to worship Albert, and was more concerned with the possibility that it might be a foretaste of hell. Indeed

65

she confessed that she was so accustomed to having her own way that the odds were ten to one against her agreeing with anybody. As in addition Victoria's victory over Peel in the matter of her ladies had staved off the day when she would have to part with her 'good Lord Melbourne', it is not surprising that she preferred to continue as she was. Marriage was after all, as Lord Melbourne was quick to point out, a step which involved both her personal happiness and political considerations, and should not be undertaken lightly. Victoria could not have agreed more!

Three days after her last talk with Melbourne on the matter, Victoria wrote a letter to her uncle designed to cover her retreat. She began by asking if Albert himself were aware of the family plan for their marriage, though it is difficult to believe that she was genuinely ignorant on this point. Next, she asked if Albert realised that there was no implied engagement between them. As she pointed out in a slightly panic-stricken manner, she might like him as a friend, as a cousin, as a brother but not more than that, in which case she insisted that she could not be regarded as being in any way guilty of a breach of promise, because she declared emphatically 'I *never gave any*'. What is more, she utterly refused even to consider making a '*final promise*' that year. Even if Albert did come, and she did consider the possibility of marriage, she made it clear that this could not take place for another two or three years at the earliest. Finally she told her uncle that she had 'great repugnance to changing her present position', adding that the subject was not 'an agreeable one'. In every way Victoria was determined to leave her uncle with no illusions. Nevertheless he persisted and the visit was arranged for early October. Victoria stalled almost to the end. Writing to Leopold in August, she told him that she did not feel at all well and was thoroughly exhausted by all she had gone through that session. This was understandable, there had been the Bedchamber crisis in May and Lady Flora had died in July. Even after she had agreed to the visit, Victoria was still at pains to make it clear that she was in no way committing herself. On 25 September she asked her uncle to detain her cousins, (not, be it noted, her 'dearest cousins' or 'dear Albert' but merely 'the cousins') for a few days, because some of her ministers were coming to Windsor on important business and

66

she feared that if the arrival of the young Coburgs coincided with the presence of her ministers, the public might suppose that an announcement of her engagement was imminent. In any case, she thought that a day or two in Brussels would do 'those young gentlemen' good. Nevertheless, somewhat illogically, Victoria was obviously annoyed when she received a letter from Albert telling her that they could not set out until the 6th. Eventually they arrived at 7.30 on the evening of 10 October. On the previous evening the Queen confided in Melbourne that she was very tired; obviously she was not looking forward to the strain that she feared lay ahead.

Albert himself was arriving in no very happy frame of mind. Previously he had told his tutor that he had heard that 'Victoria is said to be incredibly stubborn, and her extreme obstinacy to be constantly at war with her good nature; she delights in Court ceremonies, etiquette and trivial formalities. She is said not to take the slightest pleasure in nature and to enjoy sitting up at night and sleeping late into the day.' These, he wrote, were gloomy prospects. By the time that he and Ernest were to make their journey to England, he was aware that even these 'gloomy prospects' were uncertain and that he was to be viewed as a future husband on approval. Albert was never a person to shirk what he thought to be his duty and his uncle Leopold had constantly emphasised that he must consider his position as Victoria's husband a high responsibility to which he must dedicate himself with unswerving devotion. Nevertheless, he was not prepared to wait endlessly on her shilly-shallying, only to be left looking ridiculous at the end of it. He told his uncle that if Victoria did not make up her mind one way or the other he would withdraw from the lists. Perhaps at this stage he would have been slightly relieved to do so. What kind of a young man, or 'young gentleman' as his prospective wife had so coldly called him, was Prince Albert? A disgruntled Athenian is once said to have voted against Aristides because he was tired of hearing him described as 'the Just'. In the same way the modern reader, caught in the cross-fire between the nineteenth-century picture of a paragon of all the virtues and the twentieth-century jargon of the psychiatrist, is inclined to the view that 'He couldn't be, but if he were he must have paid for it!' Possibly the layman's short answer is 'He was and he did!'

> '*Victoria is said to be incredibly stubborn, and her extreme obstinacy to be constantly at war with her good nature*'

In his early years Albert seems to have been a merry but over-sensitive child with a tendency to introspection. His childish sense of security had been shattered when his pretty young mother, neglected by a selfish, unfaithful husband, ran away with another man and was divorced by her husband. After the age of four Albert never saw her again. When he was five he started to keep a diary, in which he recorded his nervous fears and frequent tears. Fortunately there were many compensations in his boyhood. His grandmother, the Duchess Sophia, was an intelligent and sensible woman who lavished an understanding affection on her young grandson. Also Albert adored his elder brother Ernest, who was a much more robust and earthy character, cast more in his father's mould. Their young days were spent together, first at the charming castle at Rosenau, which throughout the Prince's life held a very special place in his affections, and later when the brothers were pursuing their studies, first at Brussels and then at the university of Bonn. When the time came for their paths to divide, the break was a painful one, Albert writing mournfully that during all the years of their early life they had never been separated for a single day. All his life he retained a tender love for his brother, who in many ways was by no means an admirable character. Albert's boyhood and student days were, in contrast to Victoria's girlhood, happy years during which he was able to develop his natural bent. At heart he was a countryman, whose hobbies included gardening and botany. He had an orderly mind with an inclination towards scientific interests, both of which tendencies found a vent in the collection and arrangement of his specimens. He was a good rider, and later his unexpected prowess in the hunting field did more to win him the regard of the English aristocracy than he had ever achieved as a result of his more solid qualities. He was also a good shot and at Balmoral one of his pleasures was to be deer stalking. Neither his physical recreations nor his scientific interests were allowed to swamp his great love for music, particularly the organ, which he loved to play and which gave him the outlet that satisfied his spiritual needs. In spite of this serious side he had a fund of rather simple gaiety. He was a good mimic, and was not above playing practical jokes, particularly among his men friends in his student days. At meals he was often a merry and amusing

Satire on Albert's seasickness: drawing made on his first trip to Scotland in 1842.

companion. But what distinguished him most and shines out from the various descriptions of his friends, was his 'goodness'. He was kind, gentle, patient and loyal. He might have been a happier man, and might have lived longer, if his tutor, Leopold and Stockmar had not so worked on these qualities as to produce an enlarged conscience which helped to kill him.

When Ernest and Albert arrived at Windsor, weary and travel-stained after a bad crossing (Albert, unlike Victoria, was always a wretched sailor), because they had arrived ahead of their baggage and therefore had no dress clothes, they did not dine with the Queen that night, though Lord Melbourne very sensibly thought that they still ought to have done so. After dinner Victoria presented them to Lord Melbourne and the rest of the company. The Queen sat, as was her custom, on the sofa with Albert seated opposite her. The Queen was always susceptible to good looks and at the sight of Albert her frozen dread disappeared. She wrote in her journal that night 'Albert is beautiful' and once again they were described as 'my 2 dear cousins'. Leopold must have been much relieved to receive a letter, which Victoria found time to write on the 12th, telling him that she found Albert 'very fascinating' and praising his beauty, his unaffected manner and his amiability, adding with a complete *volte-face* that she was very happy to have them there. Her journal for the 11th contained a catalogue of his charms. He was 'excessively handsome', had 'such beautiful blue eyes, and exquisite nose, and such a pretty mouth with delicate moustachios and slight but very slight whiskers; a beautiful figure, broad in the shoulder and a fine waist'. Victoria was in a fair way to being in love.

The next few days only deepened her emotion. The young pair danced together, though Victoria did not go so far as to waltz with the man whom, by now, she had almost decided to marry. They rode together. Victoria now even promoted 'dearest Albert' to sitting beside her on the sofa. By the 13th she told Lord Melbourne that she had changed her mind about marrying, but could not yet make up her mind to come to a definite decision, though she realised that she must do so soon. Lord Melbourne, ever cautious, advised waiting another week, while agreeing that the Prince was a very fine, good-looking young man. Next day Victoria told the Prime Minister that she had decided to marry Albert, but when they came to discuss the date she showed her last traces of hesitation and suggested that it might be well to wait a year. Lord Melbourne did not agree. He thought that difficulties could only arise through waiting and that the public would be relieved to hear that she was to marry. Once again he asked her if she would not prefer the marriage to take place immediately, once again she refused. He then suggested that the ceremony might take place in January or February, which would give Parliament the necessary time to make arrangements for the Prince's allowance and status. Then came the awkward question as to how the Queen was to tell Albert of her decision, as etiquette would not allow him to propose to her. When these details had been finally settled, Victoria confessed to feeling very happy. It was a decision she was never to regret.

Next day the Prince was summoned to the closet, where Victoria plucked up her courage to tell him that it would make her 'too happy' if he would consent to marry her, and the cousins then embraced. Victoria wrote in her journal that night that it was the brightest, happiest moment of her life and that Albert seemed so happy and was so kind and affectionate. The die had been cast. After the uncertainties of the last few months it must have been a relief to both of them to have come to a decision. Albert's reactions give the impression more of a mood of sober happiness than of a young man swept off his feet by love. He was plainly touched by Victoria's obvious devotion. He wrote to his old tutor Florschutz that he was at a loss to believe 'that such affection should be shown to me' and wrote of his future wife as being 'so good and kind to me'. He had, he declared, attained the height of his desires; then came the ad-mission, 'Alas my days in my beloved home are numbered.' Of Victoria's feelings there is no doubt, she was deeply, but not always quite understandingly, in love. That this change of heart should have been so rapid is not really surprising. More than once since her accession, the Queen had shown a desire for some young company, declaring that, because she lived so much with people older than herself, she often forgot that she was herself still young. Albert's coming filled a gap in her life which she had only half-realised. For a month, until the cousins

'Albert will you marry me?'

Lithograph showing Victoria's proposal to Albert on 15 October 1839.

departed on 14 November, Albert and Victoria danced and rode and made music together. But though Victoria was a young woman of twenty and deeply in love, she was also a Queen, and as such her forthcoming marriage brought much business in its train. As Queen she had first to inform her nearest relations and then in person to announce the fact to her Privy Council. Then there was the question of whether her husband should be given an English title, and of negotiating with Parliament the amount of the annuity to be granted him. There was also the problem of the composition of his household. All these matters filled the months between the engagement and the marriage with much troublesome business.

Leopold was in favour of the Prince becoming a peer, but both the Queen and Melbourne, who were well aware of the widespread dislike of foreigners entertained by the English, considered this unwise, particularly as an English title would involve the Prince taking his seat in the House of Lords. Any attempt, or even the mere appearance of an attempt to play a part in the political life of the country would lead to dislike and resentment. So deep-seated was this insular attitude towards a foreign husband for the Queen, that it was not until 1857 that Victoria took the step of issuing the letters patent by which he became Prince Consort, though by then he had become in fact, though not in theory, co-ruler with the Queen. This dislike showed itself again when the question of the Prince's annuity was raised in Parliament. When Prince Leopold had married the Princess Charlotte, then heiress to the throne, he had been granted £50,000 a year, and naturally Victoria expected Parliament to make the same provision for her husband. Instead he was voted only £30,000. The news of the wrangling in England over his settlement and about the question of his precedence over royal dukes caused Albert much unhappiness, and Leopold had to report that he was looking wan and melancholy. Much of the trouble rose out of the conflict of the political parties. The Tories were using the Prince to score off Melbourne, and to some extent off his Whig Queen. Their intransigence was political, not personal. King Leopold had earlier commented on the violence of English politics, and on the practice of politicians calling their opponents such names as blockheads, wretches, rogues, fools and any other term of

'Poor dear Albert, how cruelly are they ill-using that dearest angel! Monsters! you Tories shall be punished'

abuse that occurred to them. Foreigners, less familiar with England than Leopold, often found it difficult, then as now, to realise that the sovereign and the ministry could do little to restrain a freedom of expression, both in Parliamant and in the Press, which would have been forbidden in a country whose political traditions were different. No wonder that Albert told Prince Lowenstein that his future lot was brilliant, but also plentifully strewn with thorns. Victoria was furious when Parliament refused to grant the Prince precedence over the royal dukes and slashed the customary allowance for the Queen's husband, but she was also helpless.

Nevertheless she too was responsible for some of her future husband's low spirits. It was natural that Albert, deeply attached as he was to his home and his family, should dread leaving them for a country that was strange and for the moment unfriendly. It was also natural that he should want at least some of his new household to be chosen from among his old and trusted friends. After the Bedchamber crisis, Victoria above all should have been able to appreciate his feelings on this, but, though her political instincts were sound, she did show a certain insensitivity in handling him. Both she and Melbourne, conscious of the English dislike of foreigners, knew that to include a number of Germans in the Prince's household would create a bad impression and give the hated Tories fresh ground for criticism. Albert, therefore, must have an all-English household. The political situation made it also seem desirable that the choice of its members should not be left to the Prince. It would be extremely awkward if he should appoint some who were Tories, however congenial they might be to him as people. The Court must never seem to speak with two voices; it was essential that the Prince's household should be of the same political complexion as the Queen's. Moreover, it was important that, as the Queen's husband and a foreigner, Albert should not give even the appearance of meddling in domestic politics, therefore active politicians were debarred from becoming members of the Prince's household. Considerations such as these made it imperative that the household should be chosen by someone familiar with all the nuances and niceties of English political and family connections. This was so clear to Victoria that she seemed inclined to underestimate Albert's reactions

The marriage of Victoria and Albert, which took place on 10 February 1840 in the Chapel Royal, St James's Palace. Painting by George Hayter.

and not to realise that the tone of her letters might wound a sensitive person. For instance, Albert wrote pointing out that 'If I am really to keep myself free from all parties, my people must not belong exclusively to one side. ... It is very necessary that they should be chosen from both sides ... the same number of Whigs as of Tories.' The Prince was also insistent that 'they should be men well educated and of high character'. The Queen replied blandly that his ideas would not do at all, though she promised that the men chosen for him would be respectable, distinguished persons of high character. Apparently some of the Prince's disquiet was due to the rumours that had circulated after the Lady Flora affair that the reputation of some of the people surrounding the Queen was open to question. Meanwhile Victoria and Melbourne had decided that George Anson, who was already Lord Melbourne's private secretary, should act in that capacity for the Prince. Again Albert protested against having a man about whom he knew nothing placed in so confidential a post and again Victoria rejected his plea, while sugaring the pill by assuring him that it was her greatest and most anxious wish to arrange matters to his liking. Nevertheless Anson was to become his private secretary. In reply Albert, while expressing his disappointment, gave a reluctant consent to the arrangements that Victoria was making for him, declaring his confidence in her judgment. The interest of this correspondence is in the way in which it reveals the footing on which the partners to the forthcoming wedding stood in the months before it took place. Victoria adored Albert but never once did she allow her feelings to cloud her judgment as Queen. In all these matters Victoria had acted in close co-operation with Melbourne, and it was generous of Albert to write to the Prime Minister thanking him for all the trouble he had taken. In another man the gesture might have been ironical. One wonders if the Prince had smiled a little wryly when Victoria wrote to her dearest Albert telling him how happy she would be if he would be very friendly to 'this good and just man'.

On Saturday 8 February, Albert arrived with his brother and father and two days later he and Victoria were married. The bride wore a white satin gown with a deep flounce of Honiton lace, her Turkish diamond necklace, and a sapphire brooch that Albert had given her. It was a relief, after the coldness of the public towards her over Lady Flora's death, to be cheered enthusiastically by the crowds in St James's Park and again on the return journey from the Chapel Royal. After the wedding breakfast, the bride changed into her going-away dress, a white silk gown trimmed with swansdown, which she wore with a bonnet adorned with orange blossom. There was a last kind look from Lord Melbourne as she pressed his hand in farewell, and then the young pair departed in their coach, for Windsor. At last it was 'I and Albert alone'. They must have made a charming couple, he so tall and handsome, she so tiny, so graceful and so adoring. They were both young and had much to learn. It was not easy to marry a Queen, nor was it easy to be both a Queen and a loving wife and mother before the days of female emancipation.

Next morning Victoria found time to dash off a short letter to her uncle telling him how happy she was, 'the happiest, happiest Being that ever existed' and that Albert was 'an Angel and his kindness and affection for me is really touching. To look into those dear eyes and that dear sunny face, is enough to make me adore him.' In her role as wife Victoria found complete fulfilment. Her journal, her letters, even her public speeches, abound with endearing terms; he was an angel and the fount of all wisdom – it was clear that she was deeply in love. Whether

Albert was as lyrically happy as his wife proclaimed herself to be has been questioned both by contemporaries – the Duchess of Bedford thought he was not a bit in love with his wife – and by subsequent biographers, such as Lytton Strachey. It is presumptuous of either to pontificate on the subject. Who, discussing the marriage of even close friends, can genuinely know their inmost and private feelings towards one another? Nevertheless the subject continues to fascinate. On the evidence of the Prince's letters to Victoria, both before and after their marriage, when for any reason they were apart, their love was mutual. Amid all the strains of their engagement Albert wrote to her 'while I possess your love they cannot make me unhappy'. After the wedding he wrote to his ex-tutor 'I could wish for no happier family life than has been granted to me', and later still to his brother, 'I wish you could be here and see in us a couple united in love and unanimity … be as happy as we are; more I cannot wish for you '

What a man writes, both to his wife and to his friends, cannot always be taken as unquestioned evidence as to his inmost, and often unconfessed feelings. Albert was convinced of the moral sanctity of marriage. In the letter to Ernest quoted above, he also wrote 'a married couple must be chained to one another, be inseparable and live only for one another'. His views on sexual licence were strict. He had seen too much of its evils in his own home – where his father had been a libertine, his mother a neglected wife who had finally run away with another man – and his brother was plainly treading the same path as his father. In Albert's own case his tutor, Leopold and finally Stockmar had all fostered his sense of duty to almost abnormal lengths and undoubtedly he believed that it was a man's duty to love his wife. Moreover, in spite of her temperamental defects, Victoria was in many ways a lovable young woman. Stockmar described her as 'always quick and acute in her perceptions; straightforward, moreover of a singular purity of heart, without a trace of vanity or pretension. She will consequently do full justice to the Prince's head and heart.' Predisposed as Albert was to be a devoted husband, Victoria's near worship of him must have made it easy for him to feel that he reciprocated her love. Perhaps fortunately for them both, Albert was never tempted to be unfaithful, even in his heart, to his marriage vows. He was

'While I possess your love they cannot make me unhappy'

a man more at home in the company of fellow men than in that of women, who, unless they were members of his family circle, made him feel shy and ill at ease. At the same time, from his childhood, there had always been at least one woman in his life to whom he was able to turn for affection and sympathy. In his Coburg days this need had been satisfied first by his grandmother and then by his step-mother. Albert was the type of man who needed a family, with its relationships. It compensated him for the stiffness and reserve which, as a foreign prince and the Queen's husband, he thought it necessary to preserve with all but his family and a few close friends.

His domestic pleasures were simple, reading aloud or making music with Victoria in the evenings, romping with the children, going on family expeditions in the summer, tobogganing and skating in the winter – he was nearly drowned when the ice gave way one February morning when he was skating on the ornamental water at Buckingham Palace. He loved all the activities that go to make a family life and it is to him that modern generations of children owe the pleasure of the Christmas tree with its presents. Though not the first to introduce the practice, Albert imported this custom from his homeland and made it popular. He was a family man, too, in that he enjoyed enlarging and rebuilding the family home and laying out its gardens. Gradually he imbued Victoria with his tastes, though she continued to love and often to visit the theatre, and together they created a happy family environment in their two most personal homes, Osborne and Balmoral. There is no evidence to suggest that had Albert married a different woman he would ever have been capable of the passionate emotion and jealous devotion that devoured Victoria. He told his brother that he was willing to give up everything for Victoria, and he certainly worked himself into an early grave as a result of his unremitting labours on her behalf in her capacity as Queen – though whether this was due to love or duty who can say? He certainly gave her every token of tenderness. Victoria, after his death, was to recall, how, during her confinements, no one else 'ever lifted her from her bed to her sofa, and he always helped to wheel her on her bed or sofa into the next room. For this purpose he would come instantly when sent for from any part of the house. As the years went on and he became overwhelmed

The Royal Family at Home

The pleasures of Prince Albert were simple and domestic, he enjoyed tobogganning and skating in the winter and organising family expeditions in the summer. The Queen soon adopted his interests and tastes, and together they created their family homes at Balmoral and Osborne. One of the German customs which the Prince imported and made popular was to have a tree at Christmas. This custom was adopted by thousands of families and the Christmas tree has now become part of English tradition.

BELOW The reality: one of Albert's trees covered in baubles and candles, and surrounded by presents for the royal children. Photograph taken at Windsor Castle in 1860.

RIGHT The popular image: a coloured lithograph from 1848, showing the Queen and Albert with the royal children and the Duchess of Kent.
ABOVE The Prince loved skating, and indeed was nearly drowned

once when the ice gave way on the ornamental water at Buckingham Palace. This lithograph shows Victoria and Albert on the frozen pond at Frogmore in about 1840.

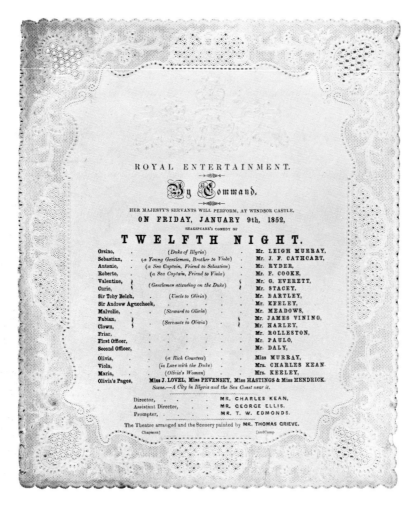

ROYAL ENTERTAINMENT.

By Command,

HER MAJESTY'S SERVANTS WILL PERFORM, AT WINDSOR CASTLE,

ON FRIDAY, JANUARY 9th, 1852,

SHAKSPEARE'S COMEDY OF

TWELFTH NIGHT.

Orsino,	*(Duke of Illyria)*	Mr. LEIGH MURRAY,
Sebastian,	*(a Young Gentleman, Brother to Viola)*	Mr. J. F. CATHCART,
Antonio,	*(a Sea Captain, Friend to Sebastian)*	Mr. RYDER,
Roberto,	*(a Sea Captain, Friend to Viola)*	Mr. F. COOKE,
Valentine,	*(Gentlemen attending on the Duke)*	Mr. G. EVERETT,
Curio,		Mr. STACEY,
Sir Toby Belch,	*(Uncle to Olivia)*	Mr. BARTLEY,
Sir Andrew Aguecheek,		Mr. KEELEY,
Malvolio,	*(Steward to Olivia)*	Mr. MEADOWS,
Fabian,	*(Servants to Olivia)*	Mr. JAMES VINING,
Clown,		Mr. HARLEY,
Friar,		Mr. ROLLESTON,
First Officer,		Mr. PAULO,
Second Officer,		Mr. DALY,
Olivia,	*(a Rich Countess)*	Miss MURRAY,
Viola,	*(in Love with the Duke)*	Mrs. CHARLES KEAN.
Maria,	*(Olivia's Woman)*	Mrs. KEELEY,

Olivia's Pages, Miss J. LOVEL, Miss PEVENSEY, Miss HASTINGS & Miss HENDRICK.

Scene.—A City in Illyria and the Sea Coast near it.

Director,		MR. CHARLES KEAN,
Assistant Director,		MR. GEORGE ELLIS.
Prompter,		MR. T. W. EDMONDS.

The Theatre arranged and the Scenery painted by MR. THOMAS GRIEVE.

[Chapman]   [andCamp

with work, this was often done at much inconvenience to himself; but he ever came with a sweet smile on his face.' Throughout his life he never failed Victoria, except that by wearing himself out in her service and the service of duty, he left her to face forty years of widowhood!

Albert and Victoria were only twenty when they married and, like many other young couples, they found the process of adjusting to the new relationship at times difficult. They did not know one another very well and their tastes were dissimilar. He was studious, enjoying the society of scientists and intellectuals. He loved the country, and liked to go to bed early.

One interest that Victoria and Albert shared was love of the theatre, and special command performances were presented to them at Windsor and Buckingham Palace. Later, the royal children often produced tableaux and small plays to perform before their parents. ABOVE LEFT Decorated programme of the command performance of

Twelfth Night, directed by Charles Kean and performed at Windsor Castle in 1852.
RIGHT A lithograph of the royal command performance of *Merchant of Venice*, which took place before the Queen, the Prince, the royal children and the Court, on 28 December 1848, in the Rubens Room at Windsor Castle.

Victoria on the other hand, was a town dweller, enjoying the bustle of London with its theatres and concerts, parties and balls, and liked to go to bed late and get up late in the morning. She was partial to gossip rather than to serious conversation, which in her young days she felt put her at a disadvantage, and in general on domestic evenings preferred merry games or Melbourne's 'funny', often perverse and outrageous, views that he tailored to her needs and inclinations. At first it was Albert who was expected to make the adaptation, though Victoria did learn to play chess. But fortunately the young couple shared some tastes. They were both musical, though even here the

Queen preferred the Italian composers, while her husband leant to the German. Albert was a beautiful dancer, with whom the Queen could waltz with complete propriety. They both enjoyed riding and were devoted to their dogs; Victoria was always adding to her collection, while Albert's favourite was his hound Eros, and great was the woe when it was accidentally shot on a shooting expedition, though luckily it recovered.

In a letter to Victoria expressing his great joy at the news of their engagement, Leopold told his niece that in Albert she would find a husband whose qualities were those she would find most conducive to her happiness. The future was to show that he was right. It was on Albert's reserves of patience, self-control and deep affection that their future happiness was to be built. Once Lord Melbourne, talking to the Queen about her uncle Leopold and his first wife, the Princess Charlotte, told her that he had acquired great influence by being very quiet and patient. In time Albert acquired the same influence by the same methods, and Victoria came to idolise her husband. Many years later, writing to her eldest daughter, the Crown Princess of Prussia, the Queen told her 'I should often like to fall at his feet … for I feel how unworthy I must be of one so great and so perfect as he.' But though Victoria had always adored her husband, that did not necessarily make her easy to live with, a fact of which she was all too conscious herself. Though Victoria was physically robust, she was often excitable and irritable and suffered from moods of nervous depression. As she also possessed a hot and passionate temper, when she flew into a rage on one of her bad days, she was quite capable of hurling accusations and suspicions at her 'dear Angel', though she bitterly regretted these outbursts later. At times she was almost hysterical, and because both she and her contemporaries believed that her grandfather, George III, had died insane, a diagnosis which modern doctors have questioned, she was haunted by the fear that if pushed too far her reason also might go. Albert, her doctors and many of her ministers also shared this fear, which made them doubly apprehensive of her sudden rages.

Throughout their marriage, there must have been times when Albert's patience was sorely tried. He probably never quite understood her need for some outlet for her nervous tension, though he did his best to help her to control her out-

OPPOSITE, ABOVE Queen Victoria's private sitting room at Windsor Castle, crammed with ornaments, photographs, portraits and mementoes. Landseer's painting of *Windsor Castle in modern times* (reproduced on pp 50-1) is shown hanging on the wall to the left of the chimneypiece.

BELOW The Queen's sitting room at Osborne; the table is again covered with portraits of the royal family.

83

Victoria's eldest child, Princess Victoria, or 'Pussy', was born in November 1840. Coloured lithograph of the Princess, drawn by the Queen in 1846.

bursts, employing something of the technique of a father towards a beloved but difficult child. Though to the end of her life the Queen at times suffered from nervous exhaustion and the irritability that went with it, her worship of her husband, for such it almost became, enabled her to adapt her way of life to his. Except when they had company or public engagements the royal couple retired to bed at ten. The Queen rapidly came, like her husband, to prefer the informal life of Osborne and Balmoral to the etiquette of Buckingham Palace, and even Windsor. On matters of morals the Queen also came to accept her husband's stricter standards in place of the tolerant ones that she had imbibed under the tutelage of Melbourne. In every way Victoria became the very model of a 'Victorian' wife.

The first months of their marriage gave less promise of happiness, largely because Victoria could not forget that she was the Queen. Albert had not been allowed to decide even the length of his own honeymoon, though admittedly the matter had been settled by correspondence before she had once more gazed into those 'dear, dear eyes'. When he had suggested a longer period of relaxation after their marriage Victoria had brought him to heel with a sharp, though affectionately couched, reminder that she was the Sovereign and could not be away from London for more than two or three days, as she was always uneasy when she was not there to see and hear what was going on. This point of view stands in sharp contrast to her years of seclusion at Osborne in the early days of her widow-hood. Once back in London the Prince found himself excluded from all the business of government. The Queen still saw her ministers alone. There was perhaps some justification for her caution. Before the marriage there had been a widely-expressed fear that her husband, a mere German princeling, might try to interfere in British politics, and it had been made very clear to Albert that this must never happen. In May he wrote to a friend, Prince Lowenstein, that though he was very happy, he found himself in a difficult position because 'I am only the husband and not the master of the house.' There was nevertheless one sphere in which Albert could make himself master in his own house, and which would appeal to a man of his orderly mind. In the running of the royal household administrative chaos and financial incompetence reigned supreme. Three great officers of State were responsible for the running of the Palace, the Lord Steward, the Lord Chamberlain and the Master of the Horse, each independent of the other and none with a deputy resident in the Palace. The result was a nightmare of demarcation and restrictive practices which would make the most hidebound trade union look like a model of rational administration. For instance, the Lord Steward was responsible for providing the fuel and laying the fires, but it was the duty of the Lord Chamberlain to light them: the Lord Chamberlain provided the lamps, but the Lord Steward was responsible for their cleaning, trimming and lighting. The result was that the domestic staff were undisciplined, the Palace badly run and the bills enormous. To cleanse this Augean stable was a formidable task, for everyone, from the highest to the lowest, had a vested interest in the status quo. For three years the Prince battled on, but by 1844 the departments finally agreed to the appointment of a Master of the Household, who, by co-ordinating everything under his own control, was able to produce efficiency and economy out of chaos. If later the Queen was to make considerable savings out of her Civil List, it must be remembered that, without the reforms which Prince Albert initiated, this would not have been possible and the squandering of public money would have gone on.

By the time that this particular and self-appointed task had been successfully completed, the Prince's influence over the Queen was such that he no longer needed to find spheres of activity outside the realm of public affairs. For this he was to some extent, in the early days of his marriage, indebted to George Anson, whose appointment as his private secretary he had so resented before his marriage. A genuine friendship soon developed between the two men, and they were able to discuss the position in which the Prince found himself with Lord Melbourne, who was still very much in the Queen's confidence. When he in turn raised the matter with Victoria, she excused herself by saying that when she was with the Prince she preferred to talk about things other than public business. Indeed her attitude was similar to that of a man who did not want to bring his business concerns into his domestic life, but to leave them at the office. Lord Melbourne, who understood the Queen very well by then, was somewhat sceptical of this excuse and suspected that her reluctance sprang, at least in part, from a fear that she and her husband might have differences of opinion. Baron Stockmar, when he discussed the situation with Melbourne, was even more forthright. In his opinion Victoria was still more under Lehzen's influence than she cared to admit, and that some jealousy in that quarter prevented the Queen from confiding in her husband as fully as she might. When the Queen's first pregnancy became known, the Prince's position began to improve, partly because Victoria felt less inclined for business and partly because in July Parliament, mindful of Princess Charlotte's death soon after childbirth, voted that if the Queen should be succeeded by an infant then the Regency should be vested in Prince Albert. In September he was sworn into the Privy Council and henceforth was bound by its oaths. In the same month he was busily employed in studying the Laws and Constitution of England, and by the spring of 1841 he was able to tell his father that 'I study the politics of the day

86

with great industry. I speak quite openly with the Ministers on all subjects, and I endeavour quietly to be of as much use to Victoria in her position as I can.' A little later the Queen, writing to Leopold told him that 'Albert is indeed a great comfort to me. He takes the greatest possible interest in what goes on, feeling with me and for me, and yet abstaining as he ought, from biasing me either way, though we talk much on the subject, and his judgment is, as you say, good and calm.'

Nevertheless there were still problems ahead. Victoria's obstinacy, combined with her loyalty to Lehzen and Sir James Clark, led to a blazing quarrel between her and Albert over the management of the royal nursery. The little Princess Victoria, known as Pussy among the family in her early days, had been born in November 1840, but was a puny child and failed to thrive. The Prince blamed both Lehzen and Clark for what he considered to be their gross mismanagement of the royal nursery. Since his marriage he had bottled up his resentment of the Baroness, whose influence over his wife he thought too great and also undesirable. Finally he lost his temper with the thoroughness that only a patient person driven too far can do. Victoria's response was to fly into one of her rages, upbraiding her husband with reproaches of every kind. Finally, horrified by the breach that seemed to be opening between them, the invaluable Stockmar was dragged in to pick up the pieces. He made both the Queen and the Baroness realise that it would be better for Lehzen to retire to Germany, which she did in September. It was the end of a long relationship. For some time her position had been a difficult one, as she found herself more and more supplanted in the affections of the girl whom she had brought up and who had once worshipped her. It was natural that Lehzen should cling to the old relationship and equally natural that Albert should resent it. Moreover, in some ways the Baroness had been less than wise. With her departure the last obstacle to a full and happy understanding between husband and wife was removed. The difficulties of the first two years were over and Victoria had learned to combine the roles of mother, wife and Queen. Albert was not only master in his own house, he was rapidly becoming the 'grey eminence' behind the throne in politics also.

'Albert is indeed a great comfort to me'

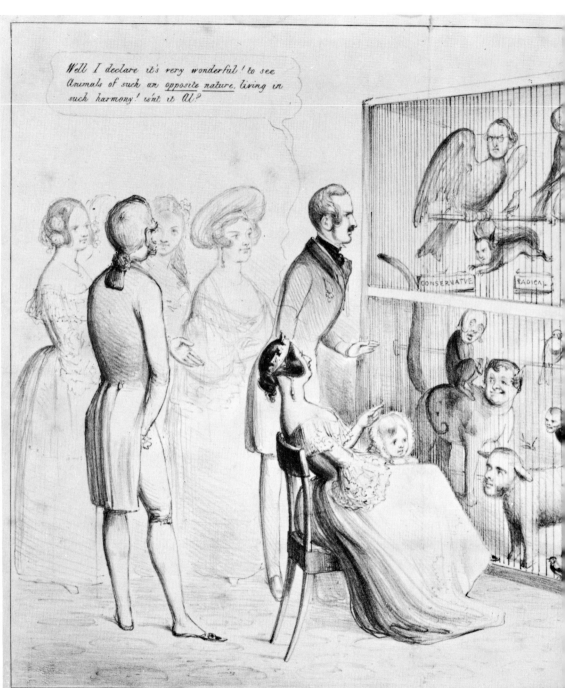

LIVING CURIOSITIES.

OR THE CAT AND OWL EXHIBITION AT COU...

Printed by W Kohler, 22 Denmark St Soho

4
The Queen, the Prince and the Politicians 1840-61

THROUGHOUT ALL the stresses and strains of her private life Victoria never forgot – indeed she was sometimes almost too conscious of – her responsibilities as Queen of England. The role that she had to play was not an easy one because, as was true of so much else in nineteenth-century England, it was a role whose functions were changing and developing all the time. Both George III and Victoria were, in their own eyes and in the eyes of the world, constitutional monarchs. Nevertheless the part they played in the realm of politics and their relations with Parliament were very different. George III had accepted the fact that he must work with Parliament and could not ride roughshod over its decisions, however much he personally disliked them. But he still had ways of influencing Parliament through the use of patronage, which in practice meant that, except in times of a disastrous war, the ministry was never defeated at a General Election. Though he was not always able to ensure that the ministers of his choice would be supported by the Commons he was, again except in crisis conditions, able to deny office to a man whom he disliked. His personal disapproval of Charles James Fox was sufficient to keep that able statesman out of office for most of his life. Moreover, a flavour of disloyalty still hung round the Opposition; except when it was patently clear, as for instance in the mismanagement of a war, that ministers were failing to promote the national interest, they expected as of right the support of both Houses. This is partly to be explained by the fact that the party system was only just taking a tentative shape; politics were still very much a matter of family cliques and family loyalties. There were no whips, no party programmes, and prominent politicians were the heads of family groups rather than of parties. All this gave to the King a great deal of freedom of action. Until a Prime Minister resigned he was expected to carry out a policy framed as much, if not more, by the King as by himself. There was no question at all of him acting without prior consultation with the King on any matter of importance.

By the time that Victoria became Queen in 1837 the situation had changed radically. This was partly due to personal reasons. From the closing years of the eighteenth century George III had suffered from a rare disease – historians are now of the opinion that it was not insanity – which had prevented him from exer-

PREVIOUS PAGES Cartoon of Albert and Victoria inspecting the various political animals shown to them by Wellington. This satirises the complex and frequently paradoxical make-up of the Tory party in the 1840s.

OPPOSITE 'The British Beehive', originally drawn by George Cruikshank in 1840, but amended by him in 1867 to fit in with the controversy over the second Reform Bill.

A PENNY POLITICAL PICTURE FOR THE PEOPLE,
WITH A FEW WORDS UPON PARLIAMENTARY REFORM.

cising the royal powers, with the result that the Prince of Wales had become the Prince Regent. Though in many ways a clever man and able politician, George IV's character had been such as to bring the monarchy into some disrepute when he became King. The spectacle of a man, whose private life was known to be most irregular, trying to divorce his wife for adultery, was not edifying; the London mob declared for Queen Caroline in no uncertain fashion, though she too had a doubtful reputation. William IV certainly tried to do his duty as he saw it, but was given to eccentric behaviour and to outbursts which seemed to rob the kingship of its dignity and the right to direct the ministry of the day. It is probable that in the last forty years the

The growth of industrialism in England during the eighteenth and early nineteenth centuries had caused a fundamental shift in the balance of wealth and property. BELOW Sheffield, one of the towns which grew with such rapidity as a result of the Industrial Revolution. The rise of the cutlery and steel industries in the late eighteenth century

brought prosperity and growth of population to the valleys and ridges between. The older parts of the town were irregular and very overcrowded, so that in the 1870s strenuous reforms had to be made. Despite its size and prosperity Sheffield returned no members to Parliament until the 1832 Act, which established that the town should have two MPs.

RIGHT The tree of taxation, a cartoon from a Newcastle newspaper of 1838, showing how the benefits of taxation fell upon the wealthy and privileged, while the nourishment of the system depended on the labour of the artisan class. The lowest classes of subsistence were left with no recourse but to starve.

THE TREE OF TAXATION.

(FROM THE NORTHERN LIBERATOR OF AUGUST 13, 1838.)

THE above Engraving will give a visible representation of the MANNER in which the Taxing System works.

The Community may be divided into FOUR classes. The pockets of the FIRST, or Highest Class, escape from the Roots of the Tax Tree altogether—they get back, in the shape of Windfalls, more than they pay. The pockets of the SECOND Class the Roots touch but lightly. The THIRD, or Labouring Class, is the source of the whole nourishment drawn up by the Tax Tree. The FOURTH Class, the very Poor, it touches but to destroy.

NEWCASTLE UPON TYNE: PRINTED AT THE NORTHERN LIBERATOR OFFICE, 69, SIDE, BY JOHN BELL.

monarchy had lost the respect of its subjects. Indeed it is often argued that Great Britain might have become a republic if Victoria and Albert had not regained that respect by the display of their domestic virtues and blameless private life. They certainly believed this themselves. This is arguable. So long as the monarchy remained useful to the ruling classes it would not have been scrapped on purely personal grounds. What was much more significant was that the structure of society was changing and this in its turn was influencing the composition of Parliament. The monarchy could have been put at risk if Victoria had not proved herself to be sufficiently wise to be able, however much it went against the grain, to accept and work within the new conditions of political life. This was later demonstrated when Victoria almost completely withdrew from public life as a widow in the 1860s and 1870s, leading to a revival of republican sentiments – a revival due to a general feeling that the nation was not getting value for money, rather than to the rumours current about John Brown.

The legal and formal division between the old world of politics and the new was the Reform Act of 1832. With the growth of industrialism, described in a kind of accepted historical shorthand as 'the Industrial Revolution', the balance of wealth and property was shifting away from the great land-owners and towards the industrialists and manufacturers, though it must be emphasised that the shift was gradual. This shift was accompanied by another of great social significance: not only was the population growing at breakneck speed, but also the increase was being concentrated in the towns, particularly in the Midlands and in the North. The Reform Act was the result of pressures to give political recognition to these new circumstances. The old franchise was historical and haphazard, and by the nineteenth century could not be defended on rational grounds. The same could be said of the distribution of seats. Neither represented the new Britain that was coming into being. The act of 1832 did two things. It extended the franchise so that most urban male middle-class householders, occupying premises of an annual ratable value of £10 or over, gained the right to vote if they troubled to register. Secondly, Members were taken away from the smallest constituencies and were given to the big industrial towns. For the first time Manchester got its own MPs. This process of bringing the composition of the House of Commons into line with social and economic realities did not, and could not, stop with the limited measure of 1832. The arguments for and against the extension of the franchise went on throughout the century, until, as a result of further Reform Acts in 1867 and 1884, there were very few men over the age of twenty-one without a vote. These changes were not accomplished without some stiff Parliamentary battles, which also raged over such matters as a secret ballot in elections.

Such far-reaching changes in the franchise were bound to influence the relations between the monarch and Parliament. Though patronage and corruption by no means disappeared with the act of 1832, it was less easy for ministers by using patronage to do a deal with the men who controlled the boroughs, and therefore less easy to get a House of Commons pledged to support them. Secondly with a wider electorate, composed first of middle-class and later of both middle- and working-class voters, ministers had to pay more attention to their wishes, and these wishes were increasingly those of the new industrial urban voters. Moreover, electors had to be organised in a different way, not through the personal influence of the borough owner but through the organisation of parties. The two great political clubs, the Reform Club and the Carlton, came into being, and with the registration of electors party leadership became an ever-greater reality. In the past the names Whig and Tory had been loose labels. The nucleus of the former was composed of the great aristocratic families who, with their commercial and religious allies, the Dissenters, had combined to curb the power of the Crown, largely that they might exercise it themselves. The Tories were mainly country gentlemen, High Churchmen and such of the great families as, for personal and county reasons, were opposed to the local domination of some great Whig magnate. Now the Whigs, of whom Lord Melbourne had been one, were on their way out, jostled by their allies the Radicals, who wanted to get to the root of abuses and to produce a new and more rational society and way of government. Meanwhile, the old-fashioned Tories were becoming a more united group, to be known as Conservatives, willing to progress towards the future but anxious to build on and preserve the best in the past. By the middle of the

Industrial Reform

At the outset of Victoria's reign, conditions of employment in industry were often deplorable. Parliament had, from the beginning of the century, opposed attempts to improve the lot of the factory workers by legislation. However, the 1833 Factory Act, put through by the Whig administration which passed so much progressive legislation, made a humble start by limiting the hours worked by women and children in mills and factories. The act was important in that, for the first time, factory inspectors were appointed to enforce the legislation.

ABOVE The pen grinding room in a factory of 1851. Women were employed in vast numbers to work in the factories.
BELOW The doubling room in a cotton mill of 1851.
RIGHT The trade union.

certificate for a cotton spinner, showing the great improvements that had occurred in the industry since the middle of the eighteenth century. It also demonstrates the protection offered by the trade union.

LABOUR IS THE SOURCE OF ALL WEALTH

JUSTICE IS ALL WE REQUIRE

WE EXPECT NOTHING LESS

INDUSTRY

COTTON GIN

UNLOADING COTTON

CARDING ENGINE

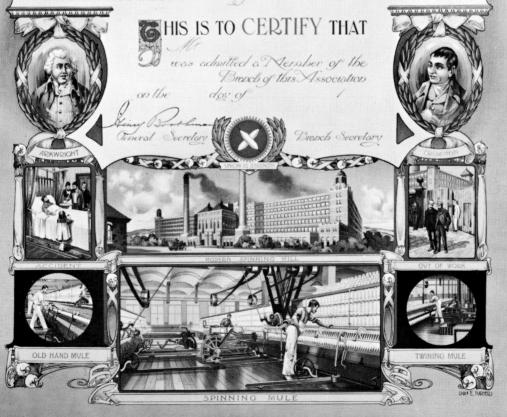

AMALGAMATED ASSOCIATION *of* OPERATIVE COTTON SPINNERS

THIS IS TO CERTIFY THAT

Mr

was admitted a Member of the

Branch of this Association

on the   day of   1

Henry Boothman
General Secretary

Branch Secretary

UNION IS STRENGTH

ARKWRIGHT

CROMPTON

ACCIDENT

MODERN SPINNING MILL

OUT OF WORK

OLD HAND MULE

TWINING MULE

SPINNING MULE

CHAS E. TURNER

J. ANDREW & CO PRINTERS & PUBLISHERS, ASHTON-UNDER-LYNE.

century they, rather than the Whigs, had come to represent the agricultural and landed interests.

For the first two years of her reign Victoria found the path towards the new style of constitutional monarchy deceptively easy. On questions of policy, which Lord Melbourne always took the trouble to explain to her in clear and comprehensible terms, she and her Prime Minister were in complete accord. Even when her uncle Leopold tried to use his influence and her affection for the benefit of Belgium in its dispute with Holland, the Queen promptly handed over the political part of his letter to Melbourne and intimated to her uncle that their present happy relationship was more likely to be maintained if he did not expect his niece to become involved in his own political difficulties! In short, she made it clear that where Britain's foreign policy was concerned she, as Queen, meant to take the advice of her Prime Minister and not that of her uncle. This attitude was, however, more a tribute to Victoria's confidence in her 'good Lord Melbourne' than to any early grasp of constitutional principles. For his part Melbourne made the burden of her duties as light as possible, telling her that it was not necessary for her to read in detail all the papers submitted to her for her approval or signature. Indeed, when Victoria failed to talk to Albert about political matters in the early days of their marriage, Stockmar shrewdly opined that this was not so much that she was unwilling to do so as that, because she left things so much to Melbourne, she was unable to explain them to the Prince since she understood them imperfectly herself. When the Bedchamber crisis arose, Victoria soon showed that her attitude towards her ministers was traditional rather than progressive. She behaved correctly in calling upon first the Duke of Wellington and then Peel to form a government, but left them in no doubt that she was far from impartial and was giving them only her official confidence, and that in as small a measure as possible. It was widely known that Victoria herself was an ardent Whig. The immediate fruit of her victory was the retention of Lord Melbourne for another two years, but it may be asked whether it did not contain an unhealthy core, in that it must have strengthened the Queen's belief that if she stood firm she could defend her own choice of ministers against the sense of the Commons.

The royal favour was not, however, sufficient to keep the Whig ministry in power beyond the June of 1841. Since the passing of the Reform Act they had been responsible for much progressive legislation. The first effective act limiting the hours worked by children in cotton mills (1833), had been given teeth by the appointment of inspectors. In 1834 they had carried out a major, and much-hated, reorganisation of the Poor Law. Next year the Municipal Corporations Act had put urban local government on a new and more democratic footing, while in 1836 a Registrar General had been appointed for the official recording of births, marriages and deaths, so that at last accurate statistics were available. Finally, in 1839 the needs of a new and more literate society were met by the institution of a uniform penny postal service, associated with the name of Rowland Hill. But by 1841 the fires of reform, stoked by the Radicals, were burnt out: Lord Melbourne himself had never been a reformer; the finances were in difficulties; new policies and new political blood were needed, blind as the Queen was to that need. One of the more unfortunate results of her tutelage under Melbourne was that Victoria was largely ignorant of the social and material conditions of the mass of her subjects, and inclined therefore to regard all criticism as disaffection stimulated by agitators rather than born of the harsh realities of industrial change. By the beginning of June 1841 it was clear that the government was too weak to carry on in the present Commons and, as a last hope of retaining Melbourne, Victoria decided on the dissolution of Parliament against the advice of Leopold. In the event he proved right and Victoria wrong. The elections went in favour of the Tories. There was no help for it, Victoria had to accept Peel as her new Prime Minister.

This time the change-over was managed smoothly. Melbourne made it as easy for the Queen as possible, giving Peel good advice on how to manage her. He told him that, though the Queen liked to have full knowledge of everything that was going on, he would need to explain the issues in an elementary way, so that she could grasp the essentials without being overwhelmed by detail. He also warned Peel that he should make sure that the Queen should receive this information directly from himself and not be left to find out things at second hand. To Victoria also, he gave good advice, telling her 'You will find

'You will find a great support in the Prince; he is so able'

In 1846, Sir Robert Peel became convinced, partly by the terrible potato famine which had broken out in Ireland, of the necessity to repeal the restrictive Corn Laws. In doing so, he helped the cause of Free Trade and the unfortunate people of Ireland, but disastrously split the Tory party. One group remained loyal to Peel, and were known as the Peelites – these included Gladstone. The other, the remnants of the Tory party, was led by Lord Stanley; Disraeli was a member of this group.

CARRYING THE CORN; OR, THE FREE-TRADE
HARVEST-HOME.

a great support in the Prince; he is so able', and that in future she could not do better than rely on his advice and assistance. He also tried to smooth Peel's path by telling the Queen of her new Prime Minister's wish to do nothing to distress her. This time the question of the ladies was handled with discretion. Albert, anxious to avoid any further dramatic clashes, approached Sir Robert privately as soon as a change of government seemed imminent. As a result, it was agreed that only the three principal

100

ladies, the Duchess of Sutherland, the Duchess of Bedford and Lady Normanby should resign. Later the Queen in her interview with Peel expressed her intention of appointing only ladies of a moderate political complexion, so obviating the necessity of making changes, which she found disagreeable, with each change of ministers. In this way an issue, fought so bitterly in 1839, was amicably settled, largely due to the mediation of the Prince and the co-operation of Sir Robert. But though the political change from Whig to Tory, from Melbourne to Peel, was made so smoothly, the personal one caused Victoria distress. 'We do and shall miss you so dreadfully', she wrote after Melbourne's last audience, 'it is very very sad; and she cannot quite believe it yet.' For four years hardly a day had passed without their meeting.

It was fortunate that Victoria had Albert to rely on. He was, the sad Queen told Melbourne, 'anxious to do everything to lighten this heavy trial'. He was also able to build some sort of a bridge of understanding between Victoria and her new Prime Minister. Earlier the Queen had told Melbourne that she feared she would never be at ease with Sir Robert, because he seemed so embarrassed that it embarrassed her. But Peel's high sense of duty and his rational approach to problems commended him to the Prince; the two men talked a common language and had the same serious approach to life. It is interesting to notice how the Queen's own attitude to Peel changed as the years went by. In October she told Mr Anson at the dinner table that she could not get over Sir Robert's awkward manner and that his ignorance of character was so 'striking and unaccountable' that it made it difficult for her to place reliance on his judgment in making recommendations. By December, after another dinner party, Anson was of the opinion that her dislike of her present ministers was less than it had been, though she was not prepared to admit it. By 1844 her conversion was complete and she told Leopold 'we *cannot* have a better and a safer Minister for the whole country, and the peace of Europe and that his resignation would be a great *calamity*'. When that resignation did come in July 1846, she wrote in terms that would have much surprised her if she could have foretold them in 1841. She was now regarding him as 'a kind and true friend', for whom as both a minister and a man she had the highest esteem. To her uncle

'I had to part with
Sir Robert Peel
and Lord Aberdeen,
who are irreparable
losses to us and
the Country'

she wrote 'I had to part with Sir Robert Peel and Lord Aberdeen, who are irreparable losses to us and the Country; they were both *so* much overcome that it quite upset me, and we have in them two devoted friends. We felt *so* safe with them.' The Queen had been particularly impressed at their ability to place what they thought to be the welfare of the country over what might have been advantageous only to their party.

Nevertheless, at least during the first year of Peel's administration, Victoria's affection for and reliance on Melbourne led her to indulge in unconstitutional behaviour. Even when it seemed wiser to appear to see little of her ex-Prime Minister, the Queen kept up a very free and constant correspondence with him, allowing him to express opinions on political matters which were no longer his business. Stockmar, who held strict views on constitutional propriety, was horrified. He addressed remonstrance after remonstrance to Melbourne, who found himself without the necessary strength of mind to terminate a correspondence which was for him one of the few remaining pleasures of his old age, though, as he told that invaluable go-between Anson, he was careful never to say anything that might seem to bring his opinions into conflict with those of Sir Robert. Even so, Stockmar was convinced that while the Queen felt that she could rely on Melbourne, she would never give full weight to the advice that she received from Peel. Moreover Stockmar was terrified that Sir Robert might become aware of the correspondence which was becoming known in some circles. In November, in the course of a social call which the Baron was making, he was told that Mrs Norton, who was an old friend of Lord Melbourne's, had stated that Melbourne and the Queen were still corresponding daily. Had this gossip come to the ears of the Prime Minister, it must have caused a new constitutional crisis. In any case Stockmar, who knew Victoria's character well, argued that the fact that the Queen had remained in close communication with an ex-minister on this occasion, if the constant interchange of letters were allowed to continue, would have the dangerous effect of encouraging her to adopt the same line of conduct on later occasions also. Time rather than remonstrance brought this dangerous precedent to an end. As the Queen came to rely more on her husband and on Peel, the content of the letters became more innocuous and was largely concerned with books read, with family news and with inquiries about the old man's health. Finally as the correspondence became less and less frequent a sad note creeps into Melbourne's letters as when on 9 October 1844 he wrote expressing his pleasure at receiving a letter 'as he had begun to think your Majesty's silence rather long'.

Apart from this lapse on her part, Victoria had not so far found the role of a constitutional monarch in her relations with her ministers too difficult. The situation changed sharply when Lord Palmerston became Foreign Secretary in Lord John Russell's ministry, which replaced that of Peel. Almost immediately there was a clash of both policies and personalities, which had not been apparent when Palmerston was Foreign Secretary in Lord Melbourne's administration. In those early days, Victoria had found him pleasant and agreeable, as when he had been a member of that happy and successful house party at Windsor in the October of 1837. By 1846 the basic elements in the situation had changed. In 1837 the Queen's reliance on Lord Melbourne had made her less aware of the possibilities of friction with her Foreign Secretary, also the diplomatic situation had not been so tense and had given Palmerston less scope for his brusquely-expressed diplomacy. By 1846 the Queen, backed by Albert's knowledge of the Continent, had her own informed opinion on both the content and methods of the foreign policy of Britain. It was in this field that the interests of both the Queen and the Prince were most personally involved. It is difficult today to realise the extent to which most nineteenth-century rulers shaped and directed the foreign policy of their states. The royal families of Europe were an exclusive society: they intermarried and exchanged personal visits. Victoria and Albert were related in one way or another to most of them: her uncle was King of the Belgians; his wife, with whom Victoria was on terms of close affection, was the daughter of Louis Philippe, King of France; one of her favourite cousins was married to the Queen of Portugal. The family ramifications of the Coburgs were endless and in all of them Victoria took a personal interest. When she and Albert visited Louis Philippe and his wife at the Château d'Eu it was more like a family party than a State visit, and Victoria found it delightful to be among people who, because they were of equal rank,

Victoria, the Guardian Angel: a German caricature of the Queen giving asylum to the displaced monarchs of Europe, following the revolutions of 1848.

allowed her to relax and be at her ease. When, in 1844, the Tsar Nicholas paid a visit to Windsor, Victoria told her uncle 'He is very easy to get on with. Really it seems like a dream when I think that we breakfast and walk out with *this* greatest of all earthly Potentates as quietly as if we were walking with Charles [her half-brother] or any one.' With this background went a built-in conviction that foreign policy should be conducted in terms of courteous interchange. Another inbuilt principle was that legitimate rulers had a right to the respect and loyalty of their subjects, and that any hint of insubordination, and certainly of incipient revolution, was never to be encouraged.

It was this last principle that led to clashes on policy with Lord Palmerston. Much of Europe was seething with constitutional and national aspirations. Countries without constitutions were demanding them, others such as Hungary, or the Italian dependencies of the Austrian Empire, were demanding independence from foreign rulers, particularly where that rule was both alien and oppressive. With much of this unrest Lord Palmerston found himself in sympathy. As a Whig he believed in constitutional restraints on monarchs, pointing somewhat self-righteously to the example of Britain. Though he did not believe in active armed interference in the internal affairs of other states, he was prolific in good and unasked advice which he expressed in trenchant language. He was never a man to keep his opinions to himself. Though the role which Palmerston had taken on himself pleased the average Britisher and flattered the national pride, Victoria intensely disliked both his policy and his methods of implementing it. The result was that Palmerston, as far as possible, failed to keep the Queen fully informed as to what was going on. Instead he was apt to act on his own initiative and to ignore even her expressed wishes. This revealed the fundamental clash between their respective interpretations of the constitution. To Victoria ministers were still *her* ministers; to Palmerston they were the servants of Parliament and through Parliament of the British people. The result of this clash was continual friction which placed Lord John Russell in the uncomfortable position of a buffer between them. As Prime Minister he was forced to admit that in many ways the Foreign Secretary was not showing that courtesy and respect which the Queen had a right to expect. On the other hand 'Pam', as he was affectionately called, was popular with the public, who regarded him as the upholder of British prestige and enjoyed his hectoring of foreign monarchs; he was too strong, both in and out of Parliament, for Russell to ask for his resignation without at the same time bringing down his own government. It was useless for Victoria to fulminate and tell Lord John: 'I was afraid that some day I should have to tell Lord John that I could not put up with Lord Palmerston any longer, which might be very disagreeable and awkward.'

In fact, while the Foreign Secretary had the support of the Prime Minister, there was little that the furious Queen could do. In vain she declared that Palmerston did not keep her fully informed, that she received the drafts of dispatches only after

Henry Temple, 3rd Viscount Palmerston, in 1844: portrait by J. Partridge.

they had been sent, and that by the language he used and the way he interfered in the domestic concerns of other countries he was drawing on Britain the concentrated dislike of Europe. Her letters teem with complaints that his conduct was 'really too bad', and 'most disrespectful'. On 8 October she wrote personally to Palmerston telling him that the draft he had sent to her of a dispatch to Lord Normanby was devoid of the 'calm dignity which she liked to see in all the proceedings of the British Government'. For the next two years the Queen and her Foreign Secretary remained at loggerheads, divided by

106

questions of policy and by his casual behaviour. Palmerston favoured the attempts of Sardinia and France to drive the Austrians out of the north of Italy, and he was prepared to give secret assistance to the rebels in their fight against King 'Bomba' of Naples. In the contentious issue of who should succeed to the duchies of Schleswig and Holstein on the death of the childless King of Denmark, he backed the claims of the Glucksburg branch of the family, while the Queen and the Prince favoured those of the Augustenburgs, who led the pro-German party. Such a policy could not commend itself to either the Queen or the Prince who, in general, favoured the extension of German and Austrian influence and deprecated any attack on legitimate rulers.

Time and again attempts were made to 'bell the cat'. It was suggested that Palmerston might be sent to Ireland as Lord Lieutenant, or might be persuaded to exchange the Foreign Office for the Home Office. Nothing availed. Finally on 12 August 1850, Victoria brought the long disagreement to a head by demanding that in future the Foreign Secretary must outline his policy clearly so that the Queen knew what she was sanctioning; that the policy once decided on was not to be arbitrarily altered; that in addition the Queen must be informed about the transactions between her own Foreign Office and those of other Powers; finally, she must receive both foreign dispatches and the draft replies to them in good time to study them. Lord Palmerston expressed great distress at the Queen's displeasure and promised with tears in his eyes to amend his ways, which he did, for about a month. Palmerston had been high-handed and had shown a lack of courtesy in his dealings with the Queen, but the basic trouble was that Victoria could not accept the fact that in the last resort the control of foreign policy had slipped out of the hands of the Crown and that so long as the Foreign Secretary had the support of the Commons he could pay as much, or as little, attention to the royal advice as he wished. Even so, the way in which Lord Palmerston had made this apparent was gall to a proud woman, who had a good deal of knowledge, often reinforced by a shrewd judgment, when it came to the affairs of Europe.

Suddenly the exuberant Pam over-reached himself. In the revolutions of 1848, Louis Philippe and the French royal family had been driven from France, finally finding a refuge at Claremont, and after a period of confusion Louis Napoleon, Bonaparte's nephew, had been elected President of the new Republic. In December 1851, by a *coup d'état* he proclaimed himself Emperor of the French. Both the Queen and Lord John agreed that England should adopt a neutral attitude when, to their surprise and annoyance, they discovered that Lord Palmerston, acting on his own initiative, had already assured the French ambassador of his support. This was too much even for Lord John, who demanded his resignation. Lord Granville went to the Foreign Office in his place and Victoria sighed with relief. It was not to be for long. In two months time Pam was able to defeat Lord John's government over the question of the need for a national militia. A weak Conservative government under Lord Derby – Peel had died in 1850 – lasted for less than a year. Then the Whigs came back under Victoria's old friend the Earl of Aberdeen. The drawback was that the Peelites were not strong enough to stand alone without the support of the old Whig Party, and the Queen had to accept Palmerston as Home Secretary. However, the fact that he was no longer at the Foreign Office meant a relaxation of tension; Victoria was not particularly interested in internal policy and there was less likelihood of clashes occurring.

By 1853 a new crisis was threatening. One of the problems facing Europe was the increasing weakness of the sprawling Turkish empire, the 'sick man of Europe'. In the 1840s, Mehemet Ali had already managed to carve out for himself a territory in Egypt which, although under the nominal suzereignty of Turkey, was in fact independent. The weakness of Turkey encouraged the Tsar to champion the claims of the Orthodox Church to the guardianship of the Holy Places in Jerusalem, while France espoused those of the Catholic Church. The diplomatic situation was confused. England and France believed that the Russians intended dismembering the Turkish empire and taking the Dardanelles under Russian control. Anti-Russian feeling swept through England and on 28 February 1854 war was declared and troops sent to the Crimea. The history of that unfortunate and mismanaged war is well-known, if only for the heroism of the Charge of the Light Brigade, the sufferings of the troops and the exertions of

108

The coalition ministry of 1854, from a painting by J. Gilbert.
LEFT TO RIGHT: Charles Wood, J. Graham, William Molesworth, Lord Argyll, W. E. Gladstone, Lord Clarendon, Lord Landsdowne, John Russell, Lord Granville, Lord Aberdeen (the Prime Minister), Lord Cranworth, Lord Palmerston, G. Grey, Sidney Herbert and the Duke of Newcastle.

Florence Nightingale and her band of nurses. By the end of the
year the reports coming back from the Crimea whipped up
feelings both in and outside Parliament: on 30 January a vote of
'no confidence' was carried against the Government by 157
votes. Then followed a fortnight of feverish negotiations,
which Victoria confessed to her uncle had been bad for her
nerves, and that she was in fact 'a good deal worried and
knocked up by all that had passed'. It rapidly became clear that
no one but Lord Palmerston could form a viable ministry, and
on 6 February 1855 he kissed hands for the first time as Prime
Minister. This was something that Victoria viewed with mixed
feelings. This time there was less danger of friction, not that it
was entirely absent, but in their main objectives the elderly
statesman – Palmerston was now seventy-one – and the Queen

were at one. Both were utterly determined to back up the army and win the war.

The Crimean War is a landmark in nineteenth-century British history. It gave shape to the fear of Russian expansion westwards, which was to colour much subsequent thinking on foreign policy. It also revealed the fact that though Britain might be the greatest industrial nation in the world, there were frightening deficiencies in the organisation of her army. The ultimate control was vested in the Commander-in-Chief, who exercised his authority independently of the ministry of the day, though for funds the army depended on Parliamentary grants. It could hardly be described as a professional army in so much as commissions were bought and sold, with the result that wealth, not military ability, was the key to promotion. Moreover it was usually assumed that the ordinary soldier was recruited from the riff-raff of the population, and could be trained in the unquestioning obedience needed for traditional tactics only by hard and often brutal discipline enforced by flogging. In such an army there was little room for the innovations required by modern warfare, which was replacing the traditional idea of the formal battle-piece. In 1850 the old Duke of Wellington had suggested that Prince Albert should succeed him as Commander-in-Chief. Had he done so, after even four years of his painstaking and detailed control, the army would have been better equipped to withstand the pressures of the Crimean War. The Prince, however, thought that the work entailed would leave him with insufficient time to assist the Queen in her political duties, for by then he was acting as a full-time private secretary, and he turned down the suggestion. Wellington died in 1852, and after a brief interim appointment, Victoria's conventional and unimaginative cousin George, Duke of Cambridge, became the new Commander-in-Chief. Initially the Queen was pleased at the appointment of a member of the royal family. She always felt most strongly that the army was her army, the soldiers her 'dear soldiers': it was not a sphere in which, as Queen, she took kindly to ministerial interference. When in 1870 her Minister of War, Cardwell, backed by the Commons, pressed for reforms that would abolish the purchase of commissions and place the army more under political control, Victoria found herself in a difficult position.

She herself thought many of the projected reforms 'unwise', but in the face of the Duke's opposition, co-operated with her ministers to the extent of issuing a new warrant abolishing the purchase of commissions in order to by-pass the House of Lords, who were employing delaying tactics – tradition and vested interests being opposed to Cardwell's reforms. In 1881, to the dismay of the Duke of Cambridge, the Queen agreed to further drastic reforms, including the abolition of flogging. This brutal practice had been under attack since the 1840s, when much publicity had been given to the case of a soldier who died after a flogging of one hundred and fifty lashes ordered by a court martial. The Duke of Wellington, as Commander-in-Chief, then ordered that in even the most serious cases the future maximum was to be fifty lashes, but by 1881 this type of punishment had become altogether repugnant to most people outside die-hard army circles. It is interesting to notice that the Prince himself had done much to discourage the practice of duelling, prevalent among army officers as a means of defending their honour. By the time Victoria died, the army had been modernised. The contrast between the khaki-clad soldiers fighting the Boers in Africa, and the red-coated soldiers led by officers who were as much amateur as professional, is dramatic.

Some of the credit for the initial impulse that brought about this transformation belongs to the war correspondents, and particularly to William Howard Russell of the *Times*, who sent back horrifying and graphic accounts of the misery and sufferings endured by the troops. As a result the British army of the future was not only better organised and led, but it was also better nursed. Florence Nightingale was inspired to take out her band of dedicated nurses and to harry the authorities into providing the necessary medical supplies, thereby producing some sort of order out of the chaos of pain that confronted her. In so doing, she also created a new and respectable employment for gentlewomen who hitherto, if unprovided for, had possessed no resources except to turn governess or earn a living by their needle.

The Crimean War also, for the first time, gave a new dignity to the ordinary British soldier. Here Victoria played a considerable part. Her pride in them was very real, as her letters

OPPOSITE ABOVE
Victoria proposing a toast to the Citizens of London at the banquet held by the Lord Mayor in the Guildhall, shortly after her accession.
BELOW Victoria and Albert sitting in the saloon of the royal train with the French King, Louis Philippe, during his royal visit.

The Queen felt great pride in the bravery of her army at the Crimea and insisted that she should personally present service medals to the soldiers, making no distinction between officers and privates. Engraving showing Victoria distributing decorations to wounded officers and soldiers, 21 May 1856.

show. In the February of 1855, having seen some of the wounded Coldstream Guards and Scottish Fusiliers, she wrote to Leopold 'I feel so much for them, and am so fond of my dear soldiers ... and so *proud* of them.' What struck her was the youth of some of them with their 'smooth girls' faces'. In March the Queen was investigating the question of suitable hospital accommodation. She declared that the wards were often more like prisons than hospitals, and that the lack of dining rooms forced men to eat their food in rooms where 'some may be dying, and at any rate many suffer in'. When it was decided to strike a special medal for service in the Crimea, the Queen told Lord Panmure, the Secretary for War, that she would like to present it personally and with no distinction to be made between officers and privates. 'The rough hand of the brave and honest private soldier', wrote Victoria with enthusiasm, 'came for the first time in contact with that of their Sovereign and their Queen.' What today might seem an ordinary enough event was in 1855 a breaking of social barriers in a way that was human and gracious. Later it was decided to create a medal for outstanding bravery, to which the Queen gave her name, the Victoria Cross, and approved its simple inscription 'For Valour'.

By 1856 the war was dragging to its end. Sebastopol fell on 10 September to the French troops – somewhat to British chagrin. Both the Queen and Palmerston regretted this, but both felt that if peace were to be had on reasonable terms there was no point in wasting lives for the uncertain chance of a more spectacular victory. The Peace of Paris was not popular when it came. It was marked, however, by the expression on the Queen's part of her appreciation of Lord Palmerston's zealous and able leadership, when she conferred the Garter on him. Palmerston in turn gallantly told her that her approval was a sufficient reward in itself and that the labours of both himself and his colleagues had been rendered easier by the Queen's own enlightened views and the support which she had at all times given to them. For the remainder of his ministry, relations between the old antagonists remained friendly, each allowing a reasonable deference to the other's opinion, though these did not necessarily always coincide. One serious divergence was

The Indian Mutiny of 1857 – the viewpoint taken by the Queen and many of her subjects in England. Victoria wrote of 'horrors committed on the poor ladies' and propaganda such as this made much of the fire, sword and rapine. Print entitled 'An English home in India during the Mutiny'.

caused by Lord Palmerston's handling of the Indian Mutiny. The causes and the course of the Mutiny, which broke out with a revolt of the sepoys at Meerut on 10 May 1857, are too complicated to be discussed in any brief biography of Queen Victoria. They belong to the history of the Empire. By the end of June, Bengal, the North-West provinces and Oudh had joined the revolt. The Queen and the Prince deplored what they considered, with reason, Lord Palmerston's failure to realise the seriousness of the situation and pressed for the immediate dispatch of adequate reinforcements. When the news was received of the atrocities that had followed the capture of Cawnpore, Victoria was overwhelmed by the 'horrors committed on the poor ladies', which she said 'makes one's blood run cold'. Indeed she considered the Mutiny far more distressing than the Crimea, where there was '*glory* and honourable warfare, and where the poor women and children were safe'.

The final embers of the Mutiny had not even been extinguished when Lord Palmerston was forced to resign. His fall had nothing to do with his handling of the trouble in India. In 1858 there had been an attempt on the life of the Emperor Louis Napoleon by a revolutionary called Orsini. When it was discovered that the plot had been concocted and the bomb made in England, Lord Palmerston brought in a bill to prevent the country being used for a similar purpose in future. A fortuitous and somewhat ramshackle group of his political enemies carried the vote against him. It was an ironic twist of Fate that he should have been defeated as a result of his attempt to curb, rather than to encourage, revolutionary activities in Europe. Lord Derby, the Conservative leader, though reluctant to form a government on so unstable a foundation, was persuaded to do so. His fears were justified: his ministry survived only until the June of the following year. Palmerston then returned as Prime Minister for the second time, an office he held until his death in 1865. Throughout all these changes of ministries, Victoria behaved with perfect constitutional propriety. The new pattern of constitutional monarchy seemed to be emerging, though the future was to show that the Queen had by no means lost her old partialities for some ministers and her dislike for others. The royal disfavour could still make the position of a Prime Minister a chilly one, as Mr Gladstone was to discover.

OPPOSITE ABOVE Painting of Balmoral Castle, Aberdeenshire, by Becker. In 1844, following a royal visit to Scotland, Victoria and Albert decided to purchase Balmoral. It was originally a small castle, but with the growth of the royal family and the necessity for accommodating the Court, the Queen decided to rebuild it and this was completed by 1853.
BELOW Osborne House on the Isle of Wight, which was bought by Victoria and Albert in 1845 and rebuilt to their specifications in the style of an Italian villa. This watercolour by Leitch – the Queen's drawing master – shows the house after reconstruction.

5 Family Life 1840-61

FROM THEIR MARRIAGE in 1840 to the Prince Consort's death in 1861, Victoria's husband was the most important person in both her private and public life. As she told Stockmar when the Prince was away on one of his brief absences 'I feel very lonely without my dear Master; and though I know other people are often separated for a few days I feel habit could not get me accustomed to it.' Not only was 'dear Papa' the recognised lord and master in his own house, he was also the Queen's unofficial private secretary and confidential adviser on all public matters. Hours of his time were spent in reading the Continental press, hours and hours in making memoranda for the Queen's consideration and in making drafts for her to copy. Indeed, in the last years of their marriage, Victoria complained that her husband had become so immersed in work that they rarely had any time together until the evening. She had, in fact, become the wife of a top executive and the firm which had started as 'I and Albert', behind the scenes had become 'Albert and I'. In many of her official communications the pen was of Victoria but the policy was of Albert. In 1857 his wife at last secured for him an official title in his own right, when she created him Prince Consort. Even with his invaluable help, Victoria found her third role, that of mother, difficult and exhausting to combine with those of wife and Queen. The Queen unfortunately did not believe in birth control, a practice frowned upon by the respectable. Thus frequent pregnancies, maternal worries and ministerial problems had all to be faced by a young woman still in her twenties, and it is not surprising that Victoria suffered from nervous debility, and all the irritability and uncertain temper to which this can give rise. She was, for instance, at her most difficult during the months following the birth of Prince Leopold when she was desperately worried about his health. It was during such times that Albert had to bear the brunt of her moods, which were often stormy.

However much these moods put a strain on their marriage, physically their union seems to have been a happy one. Again and again in Victoria's letters after Albert's death, there are indications that this was so. Once she wrote of being 'clasped and held tight in the sacred Hours at Night when the world seemed only to be ourselves' and on another occasion wrote desperately 'What a dreadful going to bed! *What* a contrast to

PREVIOUS PAGES Victoria and Albert with their eldest three children. Albert is shown with the Prince of Wales upon his lap, Princess Victoria sits by the Queen. Princess Alice lies in the royal cradle. Sketch by John Doyle, July 1843.

that tender lover's love.' How many widows before and since have echoed that bitter cry. In her physical relations with her husband, Victoria showed none of the prudery associated with her name. In this she was not typical of a generation that spoke of 'legs' as 'limbs'. There was no pretence that a 'nice' woman must submit herself to her husband's desire as a duty in which she could take no pleasure. In this, at least, her outlook was of the Regency period, and in the early days of their marriage, Victoria was more inclined to be lenient to the frailties of others, murmuring the equivalent of 'there but for the grace of God', than was her young husband with his strictly moralistic outlook. It was he who had wanted even the mothers of the brides-

The rapid and regular growth of the royal family was not regarded with great favour by public opinion, particularly when the costs of rearing so many princes and princesses were considered. By 1857, nine children had been born – in fact this was the final number – but John Bull felt that he had been bankrupted by the Coburgs.

JOHN BULL'S CONNUBIAL VISION FOR 1850.

[A PEEP INTO FUTURITY.]

" The COBURGS are Coming! Ohon! Ohon!"

VIC.—My dear, Mr. Bull's purse must really have belonged (originally) to the famous *Fortunatus*, for it never seems empty. When you r I handle it the sovereigns fall out like Jupiter's golden shower. Ha! ha!

ALBERT.—Yes, mein lub, dat is vera true, and it is no less indishpensible dat it should do so, particular as ve have had von pabby every year ince ve vast married, and by der plessing of Bob and der people dere seem to pe a like addition to our conjugal facility.

VIC.—Aye dear, and they must all be provided for. The little dears must, of course, be Dukes and Dutchesses, with suitable establishments, you now, and how is all this to be done but with our old friend John's bottomless purse ?

JOHN BULL (Awaking.)—I have had a most frightful dream. I thought the Fates had given me a peep into futurity ; a period of ten years had lapsed—the year 1850 had far advanced—my PETS, Victoria and Albert, had managed to present me with TEN MUTUAL PLEDGES, for which I was to ay ten-times-ten-thousand pounds annually ; and my " Collective Wisdom " fellows were talking of doubling that sum for them ; and I fancied I saw the hades of ten more little " Pledges " growing up in the Royal Parsley-bed ; and I indistinctly saw the figures 1860 at the further end of the bed. Well hought I, in my dream, here's a pretty prospect for me, twenty of them ! Why, that's one every year ; and I instinctively put my hand on my purse, ut it was empty. I was near fainting, when a fat old fellow, with a black apron, and a strange looking hat, with a book in his hand, now stood before me— ' Have faith, John," said he. Then a soldier put a sword at my breast, and said, " The dignity of the crown *must* be supported." " I have nothing left," aid I ; " you have drained me of my last *tyrant*." " Tyrant!" said the infuriated soldier ; " what do you mean, you old scoundrel ?" " I beg your pardon," aid I, " I have not a *sovereign* left in my pockets, that's what I mean." " You shall pay in person, if you have no gold," said a savage-looking fellow, with large bunch of keys. " You shall go to prison," at the same time dragging me off. A street musician, with a mouth organ and drum (under my window) truck up " The Coburgs are coming, oh dear, oh dear !" This awoke me, and I was delighted to find that I had been dreaming, although ONE of the

maids at their wedding to be above reproach! Later, under his influence, Victoria's own attitudes hardened. As a widowed Queen, she even refused to receive at Court the wife of her new Lord Chancellor, Lord St Leonards, because they had lived together before their marriage in 1808, though the erring lady was now over seventy and her husband not much younger. No wonder that the middle classes looked up to the royal household as the pattern of a 'happy home life'. Certain sections of the aristocracy were less enamoured.

The royal household was also typical of the large Victorian family. In the first years of their married life, children came with monotonous regularity. The Princess Royal was born on 21 November 1840, the Prince of Wales on 9 November 1841, Alice was born eighteen months later, and her brother Alfred – 'Affie' to the family – in 1844. Then came a brief intermission; Helena was born in 1846, Louise in 1848, Arthur in 1850, Leopold in 1853 and Beatrice, 'Baby', in 1857. The Queen's family was somewhat unusual, however, in that all the children survived infancy and lived to marry. Victoria was inclined to resent this regular pattern of child-bearing. Albert reported that she was furious when she discovered that she was pregnant again so soon after the birth of the Princess Royal. Later she warned her daughter Victoria, then married to Prince Frederick of Prussia, against too frequent and too early pregnancies, writing that 'life is wretched, I know this from the experience of the first four years of my marriage and one becomes so worn out and one's nerves so miserable'. Looking back she could realise, as she admitted she had not done when she was younger, 'that it is very bad for any person to have them very fast, and that the poor children suffer from it even more, not to speak of the ruin it is to the looks of a young woman ... which she must not neglect for her husband's sake, particularly when she is a Princess and obliged to appear'. In short, she found constant child-bearing offensive to her sense of decorum. As she wrote to her married daughter in 1859, 'I positively think that those ladies who are always *enceinte* quite disgusting; it is more like a rabbit or a guinea pig than anything else and really it is not very nice.' Her own experiences of child-bearing had not been easy and it was with gratitude that she availed herself of the new practice of administering chloroform to alleviate its

pangs at the birth of Prince Leopold, thus making its use respectable in the eyes of Victorian wives. She was also the first member of the royal family to be vaccinated, twice as a child and later after tactful persuasion by Lord Melbourne.

Married women tend to fall into two categories, those who put their husbands first, and those to whom their children are all important. Victoria belonged to the first of these. Though as a young unmarried girl she had been happy to have the children of her half-sister, Feodora, and her half-brother, Charles, playing in her room, Victoria was not a natural baby-lover. Indeed she thought young babies looked rather like frogs and were ugly. This somewhat detached view-point did not mean that the royal children grew up in isolated nurseries, visited by their parents only at certain routine times. Albert was an enthusiastic father, dashing along to the nursery whenever he could find time to play with his offspring. At family meals the children were present and family festivals were celebrated with gusto. At Christmas there was a tree beautifully decorated and tables laden with presents. When there was snow Albert, like any other doting father, built a great snowman and went skating or tobogganing with his children. His eldest daughter, Vicky, in particular adored her father with whom she had much in common. Though Victoria might be Queen, she was

The Swiss Cottage, which Albert had built for the royal children in the grounds of Osborne House.

123

OPPOSITE The opening of the Great Exhibition by the Queen and the royal family on 1 May 1851.

always careful to impress it on her children that 'beloved Papa' was the head of the family. There is no doubt that the royal family was a happy family, leading a surprisingly normal life, particularly when it was possible to get away from Buckingham Palace or Windsor and to take refuge at their holiday homes of Osborne or Balmoral. Today it is easy for tourists who visit Osborne to recreate those happy days as they explore the Swiss cottage, which Albert had built for his children in the grounds, where the little princesses cooked messes in the kitchen and the young princes tried their hand at carpentering. They can also imagine Victoria enjoying a dip in the sea from her discreet bathing-van which still stands in the grounds. But though loved, Victoria's children were not spoilt. As she once told her mother, when you have a large family you can administer the odd slap without being distressed at the necessity! Nevertheless there was probably less of the 'spare the rod and spoil the child' philosophy in the royal nursery than in many of her subjects', where discipline could be severe to the verge of cruelty, and sometimes beyond it.

This was not because Albert and Victoria did not demand the highest standards of behaviour from their children, but because they preferred to instil morality by example and by precept rather than by a beating. A naughty child might get a slap, a wicked child would get a lecture. As in all families the individual children differed greatly from each other. Vicky had her father's reflective mind and was given to reading and to pondering. She was particularly influenced by his high moral outlook and his belief in liberal government, a belief that later in her own marriage she used to influence her husband, the Crown Prince of Prussia, and, for an all-too-short period, Emperor of Germany. When Victoria's second child, the future Edward VII, was born, it was his mother's fervent hope that 'he may resemble his angelic Father in every respect, both in mind and body'. Unfortunately for the peace of mind of his parents and for his own happiness, this hope was not to be realised, there was much in young Bertie that was more reminiscent of 'Uncle-King', George IV. However, it was not until young Albert Edward was about nine that his parents began to worry themselves that their son was not making the educational progress that they expected from him. They suspected a lack of effort –

124

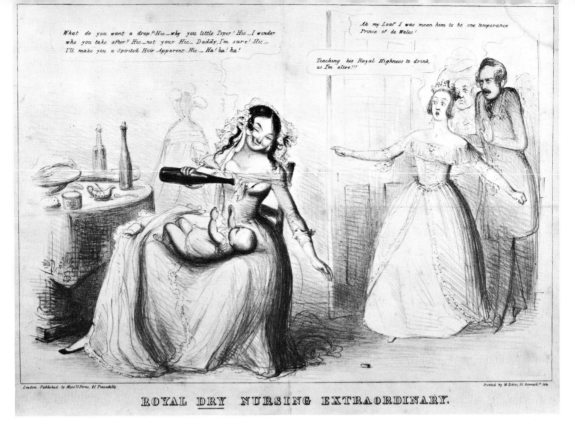

ROYAL DRY NURSING EXTRAORDINARY.

Temperance cartoon showing a royal nurse imbuing the infant Prince of Wales with a taste for alcohol. This cartoon contains unconscious irony in that the Queen was later to criticise her eldest son for intemperate and fast living.

young Bertie, unlike the Princess Royal, was not bookish – and redoubled their exertions to force him into a mould alien to his nature. For the Prince of Wales, as the eventual King of England, life was to be 'real and earnest', and he was provided with a diet too strictly moralistic for it not to be instinctively rejected. Moreover, it was made still more unpalatable by removing him from the care of a tutor sympathetic to him to one less congenial. History was to some extent repeating itself; the Queen, who had herself suffered from the pressures of a repressed childhood, was denying to her son the understanding that made for happiness. The young Prince wanted to do what was expected of him. He longed for the approval of his parents, but it was not in him to tread the path marked out by them. His virtues and his abilities – which were considerable – were not, and never would be, those of 'dear Papa'.

Nor did 'dear Papa' show much understanding of his son's temperament and this is perhaps also a little surprising. Albert, unlike Victoria, had enjoyed a happy childhood, but his interests and those of his eldest son, were so very different. Moreover, since adolescence he had been trained first by his uncle and then by Stockmar for his high destiny as the husband

126

of the Queen. 'If he does not from the very outset' wrote his uncle, 'accept it as a vocation of grave responsibility, on the efficient fulfilment of which his honour and his happiness depend, there is small likelihood of his succeeding.' Young Bertie's destiny was even higher, and therefore nothing that his parents could devise must be omitted to make him moral, well-educated and hard-working. It was unfortunate for him that these were the virtues possessed by his elder sister, and that the young Prince was made all too aware of the fact. One of the most unimaginative acts of the Prince Consort was to separate Bertie from his beloved companion, his brother Alfred, in the belief that this would be in their own best interests. One wonders if he had by then forgotten his own bitter grief when he had been parted for the first time from his elder brother Ernest. It is most likely that if Albert were convinced to do so was his duty, then at whatever the cost in pain, that duty would be done. Indeed, in 1856, Albert wrote to his brother in Coburg saying 'Man is a beast of burden, and he is only happy if he has to drag his burden and if he has little free will. My experience teaches me to understand the truth of this more and more.' An over-developed conscience, accompanying an over-driven mind and body, had brought Albert to this dreary philosophy by the age of thirty-seven.

Until his death, Albert kept his son on the tightest of reins. When the Prince of Wales went to Oxford for a short interlude of university life he was forced to live out of college with his governor; he was even forbidden to smoke. When he was seventeen his mother, writing her endless letters to Vicky, was forever making sad little remarks about 'poor Bertie'. She admitted that he was warm and affectionate, but 'so idle and so weak'. A few months later, the Queen was bemoaning the fact that her eldest son showed 'not a particle of reflection, or even attention to anything but dress', and went on to say 'I only hope he will meet with some severe lesson to shame him out of his ignorance and dullness.' To Victoria, who had always loved to be busy, her son's idleness was 'really sinful'. It did not seem to have occurred to either her or Albert that if their son had been given more opportunity to do the things in which he was interested, his idleness might have been less compulsive. Constantly, in and out of season, the moral lectures went on. On

the young Prince's eighteenth birthday his father seized the occasion to write a most portentous letter, calculated to damp any young man's spirits with its admonitions. Yet when criticising such moral exhortations, some allowance must be made for the conventions of the age. On Victoria's thirteenth birthday, her uncle had written to impress on her the fact that she had been called by Providence to 'fulfill a most eminent station' and that 'to fill it well must now become your study', while her fourteenth birthday brought forth an even longer moral treatise; but the young Victoria appeared to receive both with affectionate gratitude.

Nevertheless, in spite of too frequent pregnancies that made her nervy and hysterical, in spite of anxieties over 'poor Bertie', and in spite of the troublesome behaviour of her ministers in particular and politicians in general, Victoria's private life was happy. Whenever the royal couple were able, they retreated as a family from the public gaze. In 1842 they borrowed Walmer Castle near Deal for a family holiday, and later that year made a short visit to Scotland, which Albert wrote to his brother 'made a most favourable impression upon us both. The country is full of beauty of a severe and grand character; perfect for sport and the air remarkably pure.' It was to be the first of many such visits. By 1843 Albert and Victoria were discussing the possibility of finding a permanent holiday home for themselves and, in consultation with Sir Robert Peel, negotiations were started to purchase Osborne House, a small property on the Isle of Wight: early in 1845 this had been acquired. In the years to come it was to afford the whole family much happiness and to give them a home near enough to London and yet private enough for the enjoyment of an informal holiday. In replanning the grounds and gardens Albert had full scope for one of his favourite hobbies, while Victoria revelled in the house's privacy. Over the years Osborne, which Victoria had first described to her uncle as a little comfortable house, was rebuilt and enlarged as the family grew and visitors came. Nevertheless, it remained a family home where family treasures were gathered round them. Today the tourist, wandering round its overcrowded rooms, replete with every kind of family memento and gifts that came to the Queen from every corner of the world, can catch the atmosphere of a life long departed.

OPPOSITE Victoria and Albert made several formal visits to France to stay with Louis Philippe. This coloured engraving by Vautier shows Victoria with the French King at a reception before a ball at the Hôtel de Ville in Paris in 1855.

In spite of Osborne's many advantages, ever since the Queen and Prince had visited Edinburgh they had hankered to return to Scotland. After leaving Edinburgh, they had made a short tour before rejoining the royal yacht, the *Victoria and Albert*, in the course of which they had visited Dalkeith, Perth, Scone, Dunkeld and Taymouth, where the party sailed up Loch Tay. Victoria sent enthusiastic reports both to her uncle and to Lord Melbourne, whom she told 'the Highlands are so beautiful and *so* new to me'. After another visit to Scotland in 1844, the royal couple finally settled on Balmoral. When they first stayed there it was quite a modest castle, hardly big enough to hold the whole party. The Queen was enchanted by it, writing 'It was so calm and so solitary, it did one good as one gazed around and the pure mountain air was most refreshing. All seemed to breathe freedom and peace and to forget the world and its sad turmoils.' The castle was indeed too small, particularly as the family grew and as both the Queen and the Prince spent more time there, which meant that ministers and other officials had also occasionally to be accommodated. In 1853 the new castle, complete with turrets and battlements, replaced the old. From her first visit, the Queen had been fascinated by Scotland; she liked the Highlanders with their unaffected manners which let her forget for a time her role as Queen, and was delighted with the scenery. Like many converts, the royal family became more Scottish than the Scots. The children and Albert wore the tartan; everyone, including the Queen, learned Scottish dancing. Albert, with his passion for knowledge, even attempted to struggle with Gaelic. This pleasure is understandable: for once the family could relax. Albert stalked deer and shot grouse; Victoria sketched and chatted with the cottagers – Lord Palmerston described how, on an earlier visit to Scotland, she had braved the rain, going out with a great hood over her bonnet. There were picnics and expeditions on ponies to local beauty spots, and sometimes further afield. For a time they could be like any other family on holiday. Later, in the sad days of her widowhood, Victoria recalled what was perhaps one of the happiest periods of her life in *Leaves from a Journal of Our Life in the Highlands*, extracts from her journal which, although originally intended for private circulation, were later made available for the public. It was this publication that drew from

the tactful Disraeli, 'We authors, Madam . . .'.

Victoria herself was convinced that the monarchy owed its increasing popularity to 'our happy domestic life – which gives such a good example'. She was also delighted by the growing public appreciation of her husband. After the opening of the Royal Exchange in 1844, which in itself was a most successful occasion, Victoria was delighted with the crowds that thronged the streets, 'all so good humoured, and so loyal'. She wrote to her uncle, telling him that her husband 'is so beloved by all the really influential people, and by all right-thinking ones'. In many ways the Prince had originally been more in touch with the new England that was developing than was the Queen. She had led a sheltered childhood, seeing for the most part only the pleasanter aspects of her domains. In individual cases of misfortune she had always shown herself responsive and warm-hearted. As a girl she had worried over the gypsy encampment near Claremont, where she was spending Christmas. 'Yester-

Victoria and Albert loved to stay in the Highlands at Balmoral. While Albert stalked and shot, Victoria made sketches and painted watercolours of the surrounding countryside. This watercolour was painted by Queen Victoria of the view from the Castle.

The Royal Family in the Highlands

On her first visit to Scotland, Victoria wrote to Lord Melbourne, 'the Highlands are so beautiful and *so* new to me'. Her enthusiasm for the Highlands was never to diminish and the royal family soon became 'more Scottish than the Scots'.

BELOW Victoria and Albert frequently made expeditions to local beauty spots near Balmoral. This watercolour by Carl Haag shows the royal couple having luncheon at Cairn Lochan in 1861.

RIGHT One of Albert's favourite occupations was shooting, and this painting by Landseer depicts the Prince presenting his stag to the Queen by Loch Muich. Both Albert and the Prince of Wales – the boy on the horse – wear the tartan. Landseer stayed frequently at Balmoral and produced this and many other similar paintings as a record of royal life in the Highlands for the Queen.

BELOW RIGHT The Queen, in guise of a Highland wife, with four of her children – left to right, the Prince of Wales, the Princess Royal, Alice and Alfred. This photograph was taken at Windsor Castle in February 1854.

day night', she wrote in her journal, 'when I was safe and happy at home in that cold night, and today when it snowed so and everything looked white, I felt quite unhappy and grieved to think that our poor gypsy friends should perish and shiver for want', and when something was done to help them, Victoria was delighted. This concern was typical of her attitude when cases of suffering and misery came to her immediate notice. But her social imagination had never been trained by Lord Melbourne during the early days of his tutorship in the responsibilities of royalty. Indeed, he had little sympathy with the new Britain that was taking shape so rapidly. Both for him and, while she remained under his influence, for the Queen, the mass of the people were almost automatically divided into loyal subjects who cheered the Queen on public occasions, and Chartists and dangerous mobs misled by agitators, that must be repressed. Nor was Melbourne more enthusiastic about the merits of the middle classes. He and Victoria were both apt to accept as right and proper the pattern of society and social relationships that were more applicable to the eighteenth than to the nineteenth century.

That Britain was rapidly vanishing. The population was growing at what seemed a terrifying rate; it doubled from about nine million in 1801 to eighteen million in 1851, and in 1901 it stood at 30,500,000. This increase had been made possible only by the growth of industry providing employment. In its turn, this had been made possible by the new use of steam power, to drive both machinery and the new-fangled means of transport, the railway train. This was an invention of which the Queen approved, though later in life she developed a great fear of accidents. She made her first journey in the June of 1842, travelling from Paddington to Windsor, a journey which took only half an hour, and was free from the dust and crowds of the roads, as she told her faithful correspondent Leopold, so that she was 'quite charmed with it'. In the years to come the Queen was to travel overnight to Scotland in her own special sleeping coach. On one of these occasions, her granddaughter, 'young Vicky', who had the honour of sharing the coach, sent home a most amusing account of the journey, with the Queen swathed in white shawls and forever demanding the window up or the window down, or a drink. Once the Queen shocked her stricter Sabbatarian subjects by travelling on a Sunday to keep a public engagement. The royal yacht was also surprisingly up-to-date. In 1842 Sir Robert Peel arranged for the Queen to have her new yacht driven by a screw propeller rather than by the familiar paddles. This, he told her, she would find more comfortable than the everlasting beat of the paddles as they turned. In its day the *Victoria and Albert* was to provide a modern and comfortable floating home for the royal family.

Steam power was doing much more than just providing the Queen with faster and more comfortable means of travel; it was transforming the face of the country through which she was travelling. Power-driven machinery meant that industry could be sited near the coal fields that produced the fuel to run the machines. Large numbers of people could congregate in such localities because railways could bring the food to feed them, the coal to heat them, and the raw material that they turned into finished goods, which the railways could then take away. As a result, new industrial towns grew apace. By 1851 there were as many people living in towns as in villages and the countryside. By the time that Victoria died, Britons had become an urbanised people, with the 'man in the street' representing public opinion. This enormous economic revolution inevitably brought a social revolution in its wake. There were more and more opportunities for technicians, entrepreneurs, managers, shopkeepers, lawyers and teachers, and for men to run the new railways and docks, in other words for the growth of what came to be known as 'the middle classes'. In the towns the congregation of a mass of workers fostered the formation of 'the working classes'. The transition from one form of society to another, from a society predominantly rural to one predominantly urban, from a society that thought in terms of 'order and degree' to one that thought in terms of class or wealth rather than birth, was bound to affect social thinking. Nor could such a transformation take place with the smoothness of a well-planned operation, it was rather the work of thrusting or suffering individuals, often taking place against a background of war or post-war depression, of inflation and unemployment. The year in which Victoria had come to the throne was one in which the workers in the northern and midland industrial towns were facing both mass unemployment

'How delightful to be quite alone on board – no Ladies or Gentlemen'

The Royal Train

The Queen enjoyed travelling by train and made her first journey in June 1842 from Paddington to Windsor. Her luxurious private carriage was built by the London and North-West Railway in 1869.

RIGHT The Queen's sleeping compartment. BELOW The main saloon with the Queen's initials and arms embroidered upon the cushions and worked into the carpet. FAR RIGHT In the nineteenth century it was permissible to use the images of the Queen and the royal family for advertising. Here the Queen is shown with the Princess of Wales *en route* for Windsor.

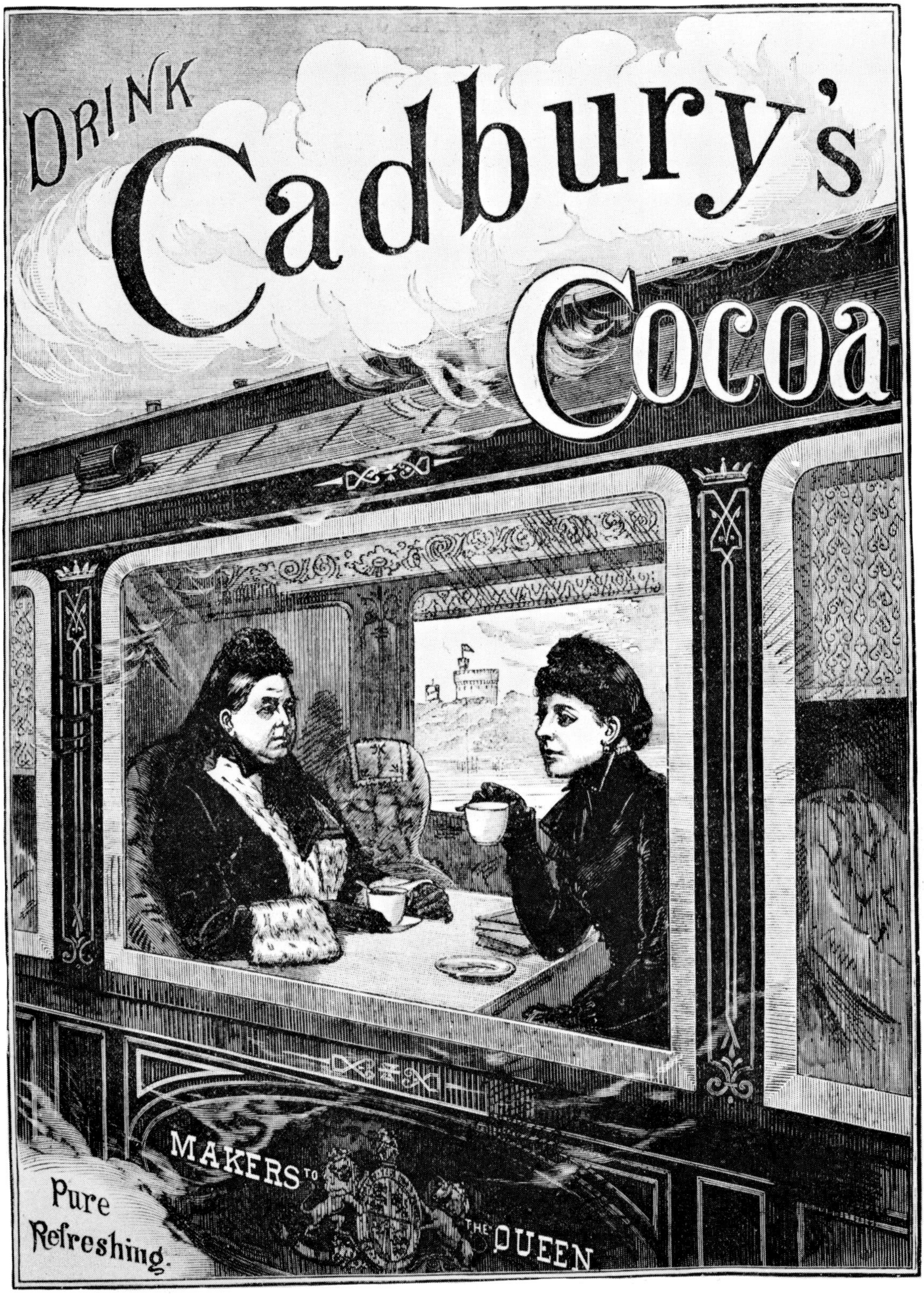
DRINK
Cadbury's
Cocoa
MAKERS TO THE QUEEN
Pure
Refreshing.

and the implementing of the harsh new Poor Law, with its threat of the dreaded workhouse, immortalised by Dickens in *Oliver Twist*. It was out of this background that the Chartist movement, with what then seemed its extravagant demands for universal manhood suffrage, equal electoral districts, a secret ballot, payment of Members and annual Parliaments, was born. The dirt and overcrowding in the unplanned towns, combined with low wages, unemployment and a harsh Poor Law were turning the mass of working people into a formidable threat to the *status quo*.

Of all this, in the early days of their marriage, Albert was very much more conscious than was his wife. His own bent was scientific – later Sir Charles Lyell described his mind as 'in full activity on a variety of grave subjects', and his interest in what was happening in the world of technology was genuine. 'Wherever', wrote General Grey, 'a visit from him, or his presence, could tend to advance the real good of the people, there his horses might be seen waiting.' The Prince was made more aware of the need to legislate for this new world, by his cordial relationship with Sir Robert Peel. It was Peel who con-

The great Chartist rally held on Kennington Common in South London on 15 April 1848. 1848 was one of the peak years of Chartist agitation, but the movement was nearing the end of its momentum.

verted both him and the Queen to the virtues of Free Trade and eventually to the necessity of abolishing the Corn Laws, an issue which split the Tory party into the Peelites and the followers of Lord Stanley. Sir Robert was himself one of the new men – his father had been one of the early cotton magnates – and the Prime Minister was very well aware of the social and economic tensions that existed. During a long conversation with the Prince on 24 December 1845, Peel was full of schemes for dealing with the unemployment which he feared would occur when the building of the railways came to an end. His ministry was marked by the appointment of royal commissions on the employment of women and children in mines and on the deplorably insanitary state of the towns. It would not be accurate, however, to imply that Peel was the initiator of much of this legislation, even though he and his father were associated with earlier acts to improve the condition of children in the new cotton mills. The main pressure during Victoria's reign came from men such as Lord Ashley, afterwards Earl of Shaftesbury, and the new-style bureaucrats, of whom Edwin Chadwick was the most formidable and best-known.

Prince Albert showed his own concern for the state of the working classes in many ways. Although his English was very limited at the time of his marriage, and his first speech, on the abolition of the Slave Trade, delivered in the June of 1840 had to be written out and memorised beforehand, he trained himself to become a successful public speaker. Wherever possible, he associated himself with the interests of the working men of London and the big industrial towns. In 1843, while staying with the Peels at Drayton, he insisted on visiting Birmingham, then a Chartist stronghold, much to the alarm of Sir James Graham, the Home Secretary. Victoria was delighted with the success of the visit which the Mayor, himself reputed to hold extreme political views, told George Anson had been 'productive of the happiest results in Birmingham'. Next year, the Prince became president of the Society for the Improvement of the Working Classes. Somewhat to the dismay of Lord John Russell, he even insisted on presiding over a meeting held on 18 May 1848, the year when Chartist agitation had reached such a peak that even the royal family had thought it prudent to retreat to Osborne during the previous month. His speech on

139

The Great Exhibition of 1851 required a large amount of organisation and planning. It was housed in a great canopy of steel and glass, the Crystal Palace, which was based upon Sir Joseph Paxton's gigantic conservatory at Chatsworth.
RIGHT The trusses for the central aisle were raised with the help of huge cart-horses, in January of 1851.

that occasion was a mixture of an exhortation to the propertied classes to help the working population towards greater comfort by the provision of model lodging-houses – the present ones were insanitary horrors – model dwellings, loan funds and allotments, and to the workers themselves to cultivate the virtues of thrift, honesty and hard work. It was indeed a well-intentioned amalgam of the social nostrums of the age. The following year, having discovered that a majority of the inhabitants of the London workhouses had once been domestic servants, the Prince was urging the Servant's Provident and Benevolent Society to find some remedy for 'the appalling pauperism of this class'. The Queen took a less active part in such schemes of alleviation until later, when as a widow, she tried to follow her husband's example. Even as early as 1842, however, she gave a great fancy-dress, or as it was then designated, costume ball, at which she and her ladies all wore gowns of British manufacture to help the struggling silk weavers of Spitalfields. In 1846, while on a visit to the duchy of Cornwall, the Queen accompanied her husband down an iron mine, where she found 'something unearthly about this lit up cavern-like place'.

The culmination of the Prince's interest in science and manufacture came with the Great Exhibition of 1851. This would never have been accomplished without his vision and unrelenting hard work. It is the best monument to his belief in industrial Britain and to his hope that man might use his new techniques to create a better world. The Exhibition was a tribute to what the ingenuity of man could accomplish, but it was more than just an enormous British shop-window, full of the products of the new industry, and a mere glorification of the new machine age: it was an attempt to fuse together utility and beauty. In 1842, Sir Robert Peel had suggested that the Prince should become Chairman of the Arts Commission for

Exhibits were brought to the Crystal Palace from all over the world. This illustration shows the French exhibits at the Gâre du Nord in Paris *en route* for London.

The Great Exhibition of 1851

The official illustrated catalogue for the Exhibition gives an excellent description of the kind of objects on display at the Crystal Palace. The Exhibition was intended to show the ingenuity of man working with machine, to produce not only what was useful, but also objects of beauty. The result was often bizarre or exotic.

RIGHT Crystal Palace knife, made by Rodgers and Sons of Sheffield. This was a sportsman's knife containing eighty blades and other instruments, decorated with gold inlaying, etching and engraving representing various subjects, including views of the Crystal Palace, Windsor Castle, Osborne House and the Britannia Bridge. The handle is of mother-of-pearl, carved with objects emblematic of the chase.

LEFT *Papier mâché* firescreen, made by Spiers and Sons: an illustration from the official catalogue.

BELOW Bedstead carved in walnut wood and exhibited by Messrs Roger and Dean.

The impact of Great Exhibition upon the people was tremendous. Special trains were run from the industrial towns so that the workers could visit the Exhibition, and cartoonists made fun of its magnetic attractions. This view of Hyde Park Corner shows the traffic jams caused by 'the Shilling Day' at Crystal Palace.

the rebuilding of Parliament, and though modern visitors may not be so enthusiastic about the frescoes that, as a result of its labours, adorn the present building, they do at least testify to the interest that Albert took in art. The enormous Crystal Palace, with its canopy of glass and steel built over and around the trees of Hyde Park, and occupying a site of twenty-six acres, combined engineering, utility and beauty in one staggering whole. It is difficult today, when towering skyscrapers are commonplace, to realise the daring of the conception, based on the glass-houses at Chatsworth. The effect was tremendous not only on the people of London, but on the people of Britain, not only on the middle classes – whose temple it was – but also on the workers everywhere. They came in their thousands: excursion trains were run from the provinces to bring workers from the industrial towns. Many Londoners visited the Exhibition again and again. In all six million visitors were reported to have passed through the entrance gates and even though this number includes those who came more than once, and some foreign visitors, it is a staggering number out of the eighteen million people of England and Wales. Most of the exhibits were British, though some were imported from abroad. In all, there were thirteen thousand exhibitors, accommodated in nearly a mile of galleries, covering a million square feet of floor space.

The Exhibition can perhaps be best described as the great 'Coming of Age Party' for the new industrial Britain, given by the Prince for the country of his adoption. It was not a public venture – Parliament had turned down the project, leaving the Prince with the gigantic task of getting enough guarantors to finance it. But Albert's faith was justified: far from being a failure the Exhibition made a profit of a quarter of a million pounds, a profit used to begin the great cluster of museums at South Kensington. Moreover, it was a coming-of-age party in a very special sense. During the aftermath of the French wars and the days of strikes, mob violence and Chartist demonstrations, working men had been regarded as a constant threat to law and order. In the eyes of the propertied classes they might also have been dangerous and unpredictable wild beasts. Now, as they walked round the Exhibition in their thousands, neatly dressed and well-behaved, as interested as their betters in the wonders around them, it was clear that they were ready to take their place in the new society, not as helots but as responsible citizens. The idea of universal suffrage was less absurd after 1851 than it had been before. The new working class was the product of the new age which it was helping to create. The danger of revolution even as late as 1848 had seemed a genuine threat; now it was over, and respectable Victorian England had arrived. The Queen's pride after the opening on 1 May was to be justified by the result, when she wrote 'Albert's dearest name is immortalised with this great conception, his *own*, and my *own* dear country showed she was worthy of it'. If it was not, as she proudly proclaimed 'the greatest day in our history', it was probably the greatest triumph of Albert's career. Victoria was right to praise his 'temper, patience, firmness and energy', and to feel that 'it was the happiest day of my life' even though her journal reveals that there were other contenders for that honour; when she was happy Victoria was very happy! This was a blessed interlude of happy smiles between the year of revolutions in 1848 and the outbreak of the Crimean War in 1854, when public gossip was to brand the 'German lad' as a pro-Russian traitor and spread malicious rumours that he had been sent to the Tower.

6 Widowhood: th

Bitter Years 1861-5

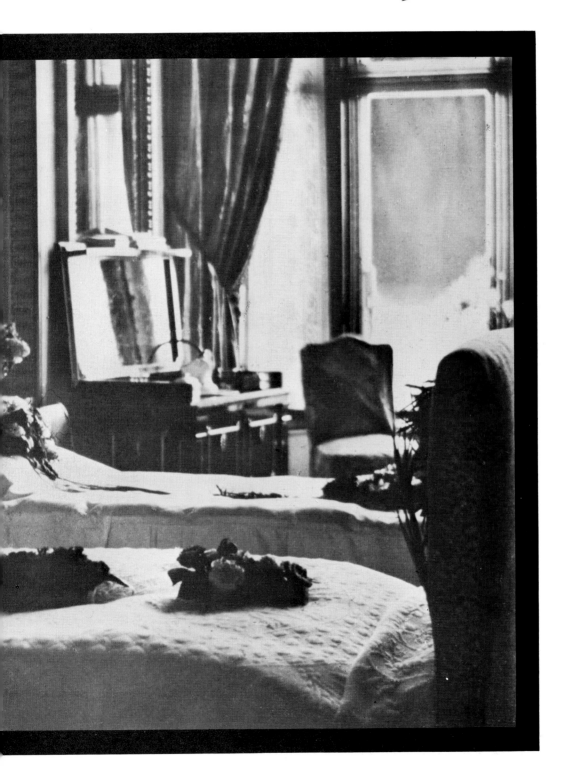

PREVIOUS PAGES
The Blue Room at
Windsor, in which
Prince Albert died on
14 December 1861.
The room was left exactly
as it had been during the
Prince's last illness until the
Queen's own death,
sixty years later.

RIGHT The last portrait of
Albert, painted during
his final illness by
Thorburn. The Prince
is portrayed drafting a
memorandum about the
Trent question.

THE GREAT EXHIBITION may with justice, be regarded as the peak of the reign of 'I and Albert', or even of 'Albert and I'. The Queen's aunt, the Duchess of Gloucester, glowed with pride at the fact that so many foreign visitors should have witnessed 'the affection of the *People* to you and *your Family* and how the *English* People do love and respect the *Crown*'. Perhaps not until her Jubilee was there again to be such a spontaneous welling-up of affection for the Crown. The rest of the decade brought troubles and anxieties to Victoria, both as a woman and as a Queen.

Her son Leopold, born on 7 April 1853, was an ailing baby. Later he was found to suffer from haemophilia, that strange bleeding disease transmitted through either sex but usually affecting only males. As the Prince Consort was free of the disease it must in some way have been passed on by the Queen herself, though there is apparently no record of any of her ancestors being so afflicted. For some months after Leopold's birth, his mother worried over his health, with the results that such worry always produced. Victoria became nervy and irritable, prone to sudden storms of temper which recoiled on the ever-patient Albert, whose reasonable attempts to deal with her distress merely fed the flames of her near-hysteria. It was not a happy time for either of them, for after an outburst Victoria would blame herself for the bitter words she was apt to utter. No wonder, knowing the occasional storms he had to endure, Victoria was fond of describing him as 'her Angel'. There must have been occasions when he merited that description, though normally Victoria's role was that of an adoring wife and their life together was tranquil and happy. Increasingly, however, public business and worries encroached on them. Albert's determination to do his duty became almost an obsession. Count Vitzthum reported that the Prince 'could never call an hour his own'. From early morning until late evening, Albert slaved at his desk. He grew portly and a little bald. His stomach was always a weak spot; earlier, when he and the Queen had visited the French King, the Prince could not cope with the rich fare provided. In addition, in his later years, he was tortured with rheumatism and plagued with insomnia. Victoria was herself physically robust, and found it difficult to take her husband's aches and pains seriously. Even

as late as 30 November, a fortnight before his death, the
Queen wrote to the Princess Royal that Papa was 'as usual
despairing as really only men are ... when unwell ... but is not
inclined ever himself even to admit he is better'. At this time it
did not look as if the Prince had done more than develop a very
severe chill, and probably only he realised quite how ill he felt.

In 1851, however, this misery lay in the future. The royal
couple had only just turned thirty and must have expected
many, many years together. It is easy to forget that they were
still young, partly because Victorian clothes and Victorian
photographs make them look so staid. Their more immediate
troubles were political. In 1854 the Crimean War, with its
prologue of bitter attacks on the Prince for his supposedly
pro-Russian sympathies, and the muddle and suffering that the
campaigns brought, clouded public life. In the May of 1857,
the first flames of the Indian Mutiny flared into life and it was
not until July 1859 that Lord Canning, the Governor General
and later first Viceroy, was able to report that it had been
completely suppressed. In addition, there was trouble with
China, and a threatening situation in Europe, where Louis

The marriage of the
Princess Royal to
Prince Frederick
of Prussia, which took
place in January 1858.
The Queen is depicted
with the Prince Consort
and her uncle, King
Leopold of the Belgians.
Painting by John Philip.

Napoleon, in alliance with Sardinia, was campaigning to drive Austria out of her Italian possessions. Foreign and Imperial affairs were a constant worry and increased the strain on the Prince, because a crisis abroad meant the multiplication of the reading and drafting of dispatches. This task was not made any easier by the fact that, as the Queen and Prince were not necessarily in agreement with the policy advocated by Palmerston, they felt compelled to read carefully all the dispatches sent to them, and often to make suggestions for their amendment. This increased burden of work left Albert less and less time to spend with his wife and family.

Within the family circle there was a mingled pattern of happiness and sadness during these years. Among the happy events was the birth of their last child, Beatrice, on 14 April 1857. Her birth was made easier by the administration of chloroform, and she grew up a gay and happy child. The first break in the family circle came in January 1858 with the marriage of the Princess Royal to Prince Frederick – known in the family as Fritz – the son of the King of Prussia. The marriage was a happy one, and for Victoria the sadness of losing her daughter was to some extent compensated for by the joy of once again having her beloved husband to herself in the evenings: when Vicky had grown too old for the schoolroom she had been promoted to the adult company of her parents. To Albert, whose eldest daughter was, of all his children, most like him in temperament and interests, her departure for Germany was a sad wrench. Victoria told Leopold that to lose a daughter was a great trial for any mother, yet in some ways she grew nearer to her daughter when the small frictions of everyday life were replaced by the long and frequent letters that passed between them. Anyone who wants to understand, and perhaps even more to sympathise with the Queen, should read at least some of her letters to her 'Dearest Child', because they reflect so clearly her immediate reactions to the daily life of her family, Court and ministers. In April Albert visited Berlin to see his beloved daughter, and in August, on hearing that Vicky was in 'an interesting condition', both her parents went to see her. In January 1859, Victoria's first grandchild, the future Kaiser William II, was born. Eighteen years after becoming a wife, Victoria became a grandmother – she was still only forty.

Next year these youthful grandparents were energetic enough to organise an expedition from Balmoral to Glen Feshie, travelling incognito with General Grey and Lady Churchill, accompanied by their ghillies, John Brown and Grant. The party put up at an inn and found the experience most amusing. Later, nostalgically the Queen relived this happy interlude in her *Leaves from the Highlands*. To the end, she and Albert enjoyed simple pleasures, pony-trekking in the Highlands, or reading aloud in the evenings at Windsor. In some ways they were a very representative English couple burdened with very unusual responsibilities.

1861 was the blackest year in Victoria's life. The stream of dismal events started with the death of her mother on 16 March. By then, the estrangement between them, that had marked the first years of Victoria's reign, had long been over. Albert, who had always been fond of his 'Aunt Kent', had worked to bring them together, and with the disappearance of Conroy and Lehzen, harmony had been restored. For years the old lady had lived contentedly at Frogmore, when in May 1859 she was taken ill. This illness, which was not to be fatal, shocked Victoria into a realisation of how much her mother meant to her. 'I hardly myself *knew how* I loved her or how my whole existence seemed bound up with her.' For a time the Duchess seemed to recover, but in March of 1861 she took a turn for the worse. Both Victoria and Albert hurried from Buckingham Palace to Frogmore and were with her when she died. Victoria's grief was unbounded and, in its extravagance, was a forerunner of the nervous collapse that followed Albert's death later that year. Writing to Leopold she told him that 'Long conversation, the talking of many people together, I *can't* bear yet. It must come *very* gradually.' Victoria also explained that they also meant to keep Frogmore 'just as dear Mamma left it'. When she went through her mother's possessions and found among them the mementoes of her own babyhood, she was overcome with remorse to think '*how for a time two people* most wickedly estranged us'. It was some comfort to her to know that this had taken place '*long, long* ago', and that her mother had only remembered 'the last very happy years'. That her own capacity for resentment had been a major factor in this estrangement does not seem to have occurred to her. Although in general Victoria was not blind to her own faults, some things were too painful to remember. At least Albert was there to share all her grief with her. Victoria described him as 'dreadfully overcome'.

In November there was sad news from Spain. Both the young King Pedro (the son of Victoria's cousin, that Ferdinand who as a girl she had declared she loved like the dearest of brothers), together with his younger brothers, had died of typhoid. It was a great grief to both Victoria and Albert, who had been fond of the young King. Later in the month deeply distressing news concerning the Prince of Wales reached them. His parents had been so insistent that he should grow up a pattern of virtue and had kept him under such constant surveillance, that when he was sent to Curragh in Ireland to spend a short time with the army there, it was not surprising that he kicked over the traces; he had a brief affair with a young actress, Nellie Clifton. This became known on the Continent, reaching the ears of Stockmar, who felt it his duty to write to the Prince Consort. To Albert and to Victoria, with their strict moral code, this was not the regrettable but understandable escapade of a young man of twenty, but the fulfilment of all their fears. Two years later, Victoria called 12 November that 'time of horror and woe ... and the still worse anniversary of those news which broke my Angel's heart'. Suffering from what, with historical hindsight, can be recognised as the early stages of typhoid, Albert had journeyed to see his son at Cambridge, where the Prince of Wales was being subjected to yet another dose of education. The distressed father returned happier in mind, having assured himself of Bertie's contrition, but the rheumatic pains and insomnia, of which he had been complaining, grew worse.

'The still worse anniversary of those news which broke my Angel's heart'

Wretchedly ill as he was, the Prince could not bring himself to leave his desk. Across the Atlantic the American Civil War was raging, in the course of which two Southern agents were taken off a British ship, the *Trent*, by a Northern man-of-war. British feeling at this high-handed action ran high, and when the Foreign Office proposed to send a strongly-worded protest an ugly situation seemed to be developing. The last public act of the Prince was to re-word the draft in such a way as to allow the North to hand over the envoys without loss of dignity. When the Prince took the amended draft to the Queen to sign he told her that he could hardly hold the pen. At first no member of the royal family, except possibly Albert himself, realised how very ill he was. After the tragic deaths of the Spanish royal family from typhoid, Sir James Clark, now an old man, was frightened of mentioning the dreaded word lest it should alarm the patient. It was not until 11 December that any public bulletin was issued, and this was not of an alarming character. By night the Prince tossed and rambled, by day (until the 9th, after which he kept to his bed), he moved restlessly from room to room and from bed to sofa. For days hope alternated with fear. The Queen was worn out with anxiety and watching the invalid, while struggling to cope with public business without his help. On the 13th Princess Alice, on her own responsibility, sent for the Prince of Wales. Even on the morning of the 14th the doctors – by now Dr Watson, a specialist, had also been called in – seemed to think that the crisis might be over. But by 5.30 it was clear that the end was near. Victoria sat beside her husband while their children and some of the household came to say good-bye. For a time he lay quietly and Victoria rested in the next room. Then; as she heard his heavy breathing, she rushed back again to his side. Bending over him, she asked for a kiss and his lips moved. Unable to restrain herself, she once again rushed from the room until Alice, who had stayed constantly with her father through these last hours, called her mother back again. At 10.45 the Prince died peacefully holding his wife's hand. Victoria was a widow at forty-two. She had to face another forty years alone, a matriarch struggling to control her family, a Queen struggling to serve her people.

Albert's death left her utterly shattered; somehow she had to remake her life without him. He had been her world, a beloved husband, the father of her children, a patient helpmate, a 'father figure' in her moods of nervous depletion and almost uncontrollable temper, and always at hand to assist her to carry out her public duties as Queen. For twenty years they had been apart for hardly more than a few days. In every crisis both domestic and public he had always been behind her. Now she was left with a void so deep and so black that the mere con-

The five daughters of Victoria and Albert lamenting their father's death: photograph taken at Windsor Castle in March 1862. They are, left to right, Alice, Helena, Beatrice, Victoria, and Louise.

templation of it drove her to the verge of despair. No wonder she wrote to Leopold 'My life as a *happy* one is ended! The world has gone for *me*.' All that she now had to live for were her 'poor fatherless children' and her 'unhappy country'. Later, when all the outward trappings of woe continued year after year and her letters to her ministers portrayed her as a lone widow struggling to do her duty, though utterly bereft of all help and comfort, future generations have condemned her constantly-nurtured grief as excessive. Such critics should try to see her case in its social context and not through the eyes of a modern world, where two major wars have created all too many widows with no emotional outlet of a publicised grief while the war had still to be won. In the nineteenth century mourning and widowhood, at least for those who could afford it, were public conventions in a society that assumed that the husband was the breadwinner, the protector of his family and the source of all authority, while his wife was the clinging, obedient helpmate, the home-maker for her husband who was her master. So deeply was this social ideal imprinted on the

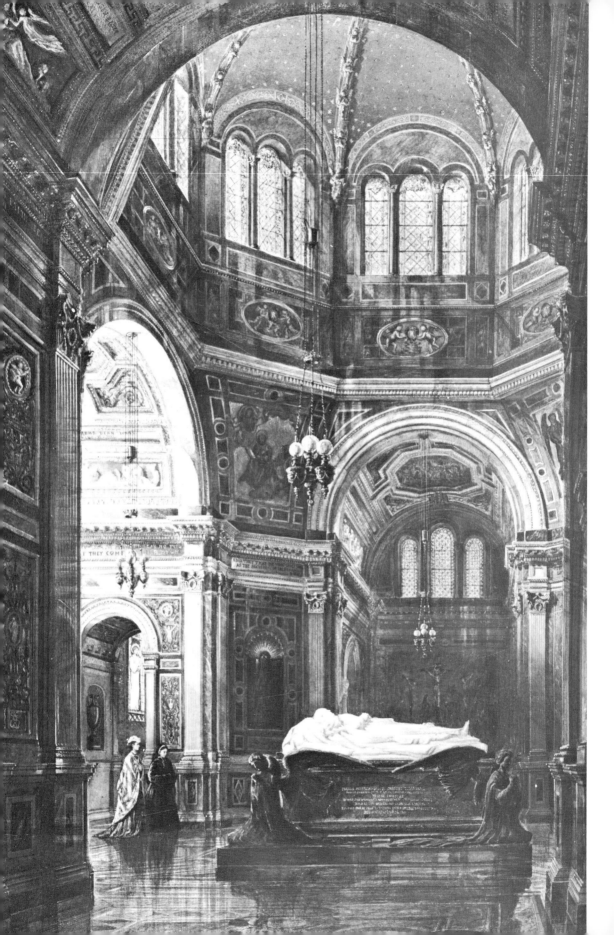

public mind, that even wives married to uncongenial or unfaithful husbands managed a decent and convincing show of grief when widowed. When the dead was a parent, a husband, a child, or even a near-relation, death remained a fetish to be worshipped with accepted rites. It will be remembered that Victoria herself as a girl had described as an unforgettable loss the death of an aunt she hardly knew. Everything in her temperament had always driven her to emotional extremes, a characteristic illustrated by her heavy use of underlinings in her letters and journal. Her emotional outpourings gave her at least some relief from the burden of her sorrow and there was nothing in social convention to make her, in modern parlance, 'take a grip on herself'. The 'stiff upper lip' had not yet become obligatory and to reverse Mrs Mop's famous phrase in the war-time *Itma* show, 'it was being so melancholy that kept her going'.

That Victoria's grief was desperate and all-pervading cannot be doubted. The note of distress sounded in her letters to the Princess Royal is all too poignant. Victoria found some relief in doing everything she could to perpetuate her husband's memory. She chose a site at Frogmore near her mother's grave, and on it built a mausoleum where his body, and eventually her own, would rest. Fervently she longed that that day might come soon. Until then, on the granite sarcophagus, lay the marble effigy of Albert. To Victoria it became a place of retreat to which she could go to gaze on his 'beloved features' and kneel in prayer, beside that 'beloved shrine' in which was housed 'the God of her idolatry'. Victoria was also determined that the country should not forget her beloved, everything that she could do to encourage the perpetuation of his memory was undertaken from the placing of a memorial tablet at the place where he had shot his last stag, to the erection of statues to commemorate his public works. To his sorrowing widow there could never be too many statues, pictures and busts of her 'Beloved Angel' to remind his family, his country and posterity of what they had lost. When Disraeli visited Balmoral in the autumn of 1868 he was presented, among other gifts, with a full-length picture of the Prince Consort, for which he expressed the expected rapture. Later the Albert Memorial bore witness to the Queen's determination that in London, at least,

OPPOSITE The Duchess of Kent was buried at Frogmore in August 1861, and the Queen decided to build a mausoleum for Albert – and eventually herself – near her mother's grave. She made frequent visits to the mausoleum to see Albert's effigy, which was laid upon a granite sarcophagus. Watercolour by Brewer.

157

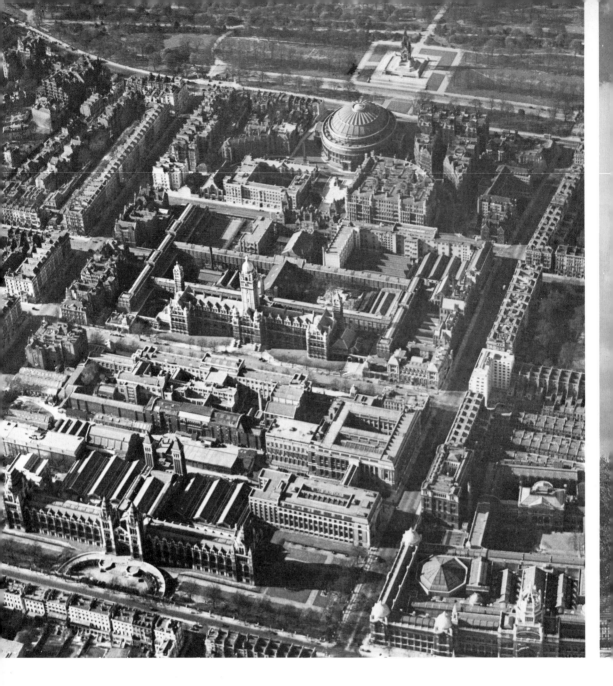

his memory should remain green. Today, however, that memory is kept more pleasantly before the public by the Albert Hall, which the Queen opened in 1871, and by the Victoria and Albert Museum, built partly with the profits of the Great Exhibition. Londoners have reason to be grateful to the perpetuation of the memory of the Prince, even if by now his existence has been half-forgotten.

The Queen was determined that nobody should forget Albert. She had built the Albert Memorial (above right) and the Albert Hall, and some of the profits from

the Exhibition were used
for a great complex of
museums and institutes
(above left) – perhaps the
most successful project for
perpetuating his memory.

Victoria's second memorial to her husband was her fierce
determination that every action of hers, both as a mother and as
Queen, should continue to be dominated by his wishes. As she
told Leopold 'his *wishes*, *his* plans ... about everything, his
views about *every* thing are to be *my laws*! And no human
power will make me swerve from what *he* decided and wished.'
One of these decisions was already in train. They had both been
of the opinion that it would be best for the Prince of Wales to
marry young, and in spite of the political complications that
might arise while the succession to the duchies of Schleswig
and Holstein remained unsettled, it had been decided that
Princess Alexandra of Denmark would be a suitable bride. The
Queen therefore went ahead with the plans. In September 1862
the Prince of Wales, who had previously met and apparently
been attracted to the young Princess, proposed and was
accepted. They were married on 5 March 1863 at St George's
Chapel, Windsor, with great pomp and ceremony. The Queen
herself refused to take any part in the public service and
watched the proceedings from Catherine of Aragon's closet,
high above the altar; she even refused to appear at the wedding
breakfast. Before this event, the marriage of Princess Alice –
whose engagement to Prince Louis of Hesse had been an-
nounced before her father's death – took place on 1 July 1862,
in an atmosphere of deepest gloom. To the Queen it was 'a
terrible moment' and though the room was decorated with
plants and flowers, the ceremony was private and the whole
party was dressed in deep mourning, with Victoria in her
widow's weeds seated under a bust of the Prince Consort.

For years to come the Queen struggled to preserve her grief-
stricken seclusion. The first foretaste of this was her refusal to
attend a Privy Council in person. Instead she sat in an adjoining
room with the door open, while the Clerk of the Council
pronounced 'approved' at the appropriate moments. Victoria
buried herself at Osborne, writing to Granville that she was
utterly unable to go to London and that 'bereaved, as she, alas,
is, of the advice and support of the best and wisest of all counsellors', it would be necessary for him or one of the Secretaries
of State to come there every week in order to keep her in
touch with public business. She also requested Russell's help in
dealing with foreign policy, explaining that without some

159

Two royal weddings occurred soon after Albert's death, and the Queen found both ceremonies very painful to endure. In July 1862, Princess Alice was married to Prince Louis of Hesse. The ceremony took place in the Queen's private apartments – the altar was set up below Winterhalter's painting of the family (reproduced on pages 62-3) so that Albert's presence was assured. The Queen is the seated figure dressed in widow's weeds. Painting by G. H. Thomas.

guidance she could not be expected to understand the voluminous dispatches from abroad and the drafts submitted to her for her signature. Her bewilderment is eloquent testimony to the hours of spadework done for his wife by Albert. Gradually the Queen began to pick up the threads of foreign policy again for herself, especially when the issues appeared either to involve her family or to be a legacy from Albert. The first problem to face her was the offer of the throne of Greece to her son Alfred, whom Albert had destined to succeed his childless uncle in Coburg. The offer was turned down and when the Duke Ernest of Coburg tried to secure the throne for himself, he was outmanœuvred by Victoria, who felt that this would put Alfred in a difficult position as his heir. Victoria's handling of the matter showed that she could still arouse herself from lethargy where the interests of her family were concerned.

The next test came with the struggle over Schleswig-Holstein, which finally broke out on the death of the childless King of Denmark. The Queen's sympathies were with Prussia

The Prince of Wales was married to Princess Alexandra of Denmark in March 1863 in St George's Chapel, Windsor. The Queen insisted on watching the ceremony from Catherine of Aragon's closet, and even refused to attend the wedding breakfast.

and the majority of the Cabinet agreed with her determination not to be drawn into the struggle on the side of Denmark, but public opinion was generally pro-Danish. The young Princess of Wales herself was understandably distraught, which may have led to the premature birth of her first child. As knowledge of the Queen's attitude leaked out, Lord Palmerston felt impelled to deliver a short constitutional warning to the effect that 'an impression is beginning to be created that Your Majesty has expressed personal opinions on the affairs of Denmark and Germany'. He went on to declare that it would be most unfortunate if the protection, given to the sovereign by the convention that responsible ministers were alone answerable for policy, were to be eroded, and if royal opinion and views were to become the object of criticism and attack. Victoria's reaction to this piece of advice was to declare that Palmerston was very impertinent and must be suffering from gout. In spite of the Prince Consort's long tutelage (Stockmar had exhorted him to be 'the Constitutional genius of the

Queen' as the Crown must be above party, Victoria could never quite divest herself of a personal involvement. She did, indeed, try to do so, but her feelings kept breaking through and there was usually little doubt where her sympathies lay. When attacked, as she felt herself to be when Lord Ellenborough repeated the substance of these charges in Parliament, the Queen took refuge behind her widowhood, complaining that 'her heavy affliction, her isolated position without her dear husband, her weak health and shattered nerves, the result of a broken heart, and of her constant and unaided and uncheered labours for her country ought to have *protected her against* such unmanly and abominable insinuations'.

This was the line she invariably took against any attempts to persuade her to perform those public duties which the people as a whole expected of their Queen. At first sympathy had been widespread and her need for seclusion respected, but most people considered that a year's mourning should have met this need, and that once again the Queen should play her accustomed role as a figurehead of State. By December 1863 the newspapers were beginning to suggest that the Queen might open Parliament in person, suggestions which made her entrench herself behind the medical opinion of her physicians, Sir James Clark, Dr Jenner and Dr Watson, who under pressure declared that any such exertion would be detrimental to the royal health. By 1864 public opinion was becoming more vocal and on 1 April the *Times* went so far as to publish an article remonstrating with the Queen for her failure to play any public part in the life of the nation. So outraged was Victoria that she sent an unsigned letter, whose authorship was a mystery to few, protesting that the Queen could do no more than she was at present undertaking. The royal seclusion continued despite increasing discontent, and the dismay and often barely-concealed irritation of her ministers.

It is not surprising that Victoria should have suffered a nervous breakdown on her husband's death, a death for which she was totally unprepared. All her life she had never had to stand alone in the way that she was forced to do after Albert's death. In her early struggle against Conroy there had always been one wholly-devoted person – Lehzen – at her side. As a young Queen, Melbourne had taken the immense weight of

QUEEN HERMIONE.

PAULINA (*Britannia*) UNVEILS THE STATUE.—" 'TIS TIME ! DESCEND ; BE STONE NO MORE ! "

Winter's Tale, Act V., Scene 3.

. Since the death of the Prince Consort, Queen Victoria had remained in almost absolute retirement. The cartoon breathes a
loyal wish that her Majesty would again resume her public duties.

Public reaction to the Prince Consort's death was to regard the Queen with great sympathy, but most people felt that she should take up her public duties after a suitable period of mourning. When Victoria refused to do this public opinion became vocal, and this feeling is reflected in this cartoon from *Punch* comparing the Queen to Hermione in *The Winter's Tale*.

her new responsibilities off her shoulders, so that they had merely seemed a pleasurable load. After his resignation, the Queen had leant on Albert. In his last illness, but before she realised its fatal character, Victoria had complained to Leopold 'The trial is in every way so very trying, for I have lost my guide, my support, my all, *for a time* ... as we can't ask or tell him anything.' In addition to the deep sense of personal loss, the habit of dependence was not easily lost and Victoria had

163

*'I never, never
shall be able to
bear that dreadful
weary, chilling,
unnatural life
of a widow'*

been robbed at one stroke of the husband who had helped her to control her volatile and highly-strung temperament, and the private secretary who had drafted memoranda and dispatches, counselled and discussed the line to be taken, and acted as an emotional buffer between her and difficult ministers. The husband could never be replaced. 'I never, never', she wrote to her daughter Vicky 'shall be able to bear that dreadful weary, chilling, unnatural life of a widow.' More, however, could have been done to help her with the pressure of public business. Much of this work, once the first flush of her enthusiasm had ebbed, had never been congenial to her, so that after Albert's death Victoria had to drive herself on to do it. When her uncle suggested that she might feel some relief in work she replied sharply that that might be true of ordinary work, but that to have to struggle with constant anxiety and responsibility with a broken heart was a very different matter. Today psychologists would agree that worry and strain were not the best remedy for the kind of nervous breakdown from which the Queen was suffering. Apart from this, Victoria was genuinely in need of skilled secretarial help. Sir Charles Phipps, who had taken Anson's place at his death, and General Grey, also a member of the Prince's household, acted unofficially as her secretaries, but it was not until 1867 that the latter was formally appointed. The Queen, therefore, had sufficient reason for feeling over-whelmed during the early years of her widowhood.

Nevertheless, there would seem to have been a neurotic element in Victoria's persistent clinging to her grief. For instance, when Vicky confessed to a pleasurable anticipation of Bertie's approaching wedding, her mother made the dampening rejoinder that the day to which they had all looked forward for so long was now to her far worse than a funeral, and asked her daughter how she could possibly be happy when 'at every step you will miss that blessed guardian, that one calm great being that led all?' This was the Queen's reaction to every pressure to resume her normal habit of life, long after her physical health had improved, and long after she had shown herself capable of handling both foreign affairs and ministerial crises, as when her government grappled with such thorny domestic issues as a further instalment of Parliamentary reform. By then it had become a settled conviction in her mind that she ought not be subjected to the ordeal of public appearances without the support of her 'beloved Angel'. Under pressure, the Queen did open Parliament in person in 1866, but castigated as unfeeling the public wish to witness 'the spectacle of a poor, broken-hearted widow, nervous and shrinking, dragged in deep mourning, ALONE in STATE as a *Show* when she used to go supported by her husband'. Yet Victoria was still a comparatively young woman in her mid-forties, a fact which her gloom and her widow's weeds make it easy to overlook.

During these years Victoria's chief consolation was to pray beside Albert's tomb in the mausoleum. In the past, her religion had been a sincere uncomplicated acceptance of the truths of the Protestant faith. She did not question the divine power of God, though she did occasionally find his use of that power somewhat puzzling, so that in her comments there is almost a suggestion that she might have arranged some things better! She once told Leopold that she had never realised the power of prayer to lift one above the world of sorrow until she had come to pray beside her husband's tomb. She accepted – as did so many of her contemporaries, though not all – a personal resurrection, and believed that she would be reunited with her husband in the life to come. She had also the firm conviction that even in this life Albert was still near her and was conscious of what was happening to the loved ones he had left behind. Leopold encouraged her in this belief, writing to his niece that if she continued to carry out her husband's wishes 'When once united, he will tell you how much he was *pleased with your* devoted efforts.' It seems never to have occurred to either of them that if this was indeed so, Albert might have preferred to look down from Heaven and see his wife living an active and happy life, instead of giving way to the nerves that had so often been a cause of distress to him in his life. When at last, despite herself, Victoria began once again to take an interest in life she felt so conscience-stricken that Dean Wellesley had to reassure her that a mournful resignation was better than the wild abandonment of grief. Much later, even 'mournful resignation' was to give way to Victoria's natural zest for life, but the time was not yet. Many years of emotional convalescence were first to intervene.

7 The Ebbing Tide

of Grief 1865-79

DURING THE PERIOD between 1865 and 1871 Victoria was slowly coming to accept her widowhood and the duties that devolved upon her as Queen. On the one hand she continued to fight a rearguard action in defence of her seclusion: in February 1866 she was still impressing on Earl Russell her duty to preserve her health 'and very shattered nerves (every day more and more shattered) from becoming seriously worse'. On the other hand, reluctant though the Queen was to admit it, life was becoming more bearable. It is true that old props were falling away, but new ones were appearing. Some familiar figures had gone: Baron Stockmar died in 1863, and her uncle Leopold in 1865. The tie between Leopold and Victoria had been essentially that of father and daughter. When Albert had died Victoria had signed herself 'Ever your wretched but devoted Child'. Now, with Albert, Stockmar and Leopold all gone Victoria stood alone, the matriarch of her family and the sovereign of her country. Though she believed herself to be following the plans and ideas of her 'beloved Angel' circumstances were forcing her to take her own line, even when she disguised the fact to herself by some tenuous reference to what she imagined he would have done. Politically the Queen was rapidly becoming self-reliant.

It was very necessary for her, if she were to feel safe and secure so that her taut nerves could relax, to have some person in her life on whose exclusive devotion she felt she could rely. This need was now satisfied by two men, her servant John Brown and Disraeli, her Prime Minister. Though Victoria had known Disraeli longer, her feelings towards the brash young politician in the early days of her marriage had been by no means warm. In short the Queen had not approved of young Mr Disraeli when he had been in opposition to Peel. John Brown, on the other hand, was associated with her happy holidays in the Highlands when he had been one of the royal ghillies. Brown was excellent with horses and had saved the Queen from several accidents, so that she was prepared to overlook his occasional lapses when the whisky proved too great a temptation. A motor-conscious age is inclined to forget that horse transport was equally accident-prone, though the results were rarely as fatal. Even so, the Duke of Orléans was killed while leaping from a carriage when the horses had bolted.

PREVIOUS PAGES Queen Victoria on horseback with John Brown, in the grounds of Osborne House. When Landseer finished this painting, he contributed it to the Royal Academy Summer Exhibition and caused a great stir, for the relationship between the Queen and her favourite ghillie was treated as a scandal.

When the Queen went to Germany after Albert's death, Brown went with her to take charge of her pony carriage, but it was not until the winter of 1864 that Dr Jenner and Sir Charles Phipps conceived the idea of bringing Brown to Windsor in the hope of encouraging Victoria to resume her regular habit of riding. This brought about a change in the Queen's emotional life. She had first known Brown at Balmoral, where the trappings of royalty had been at a minimum and the Queen, like any other laird's lady, had ridden, sketched and talked familiarly with the crofters and their wives; she had attended the parish church and dropped her money in the collecting box like any other parishioner. Personal Highland servants had never believed that loyalty included servility; they were accustomed to speak their minds and John Brown was no exception. In his eyes Victoria was a woman not a Queen, and he treated her accordingly. Her English subjects were shocked when he addressed her as 'wumman', but to Victoria his brusque manner of ensuring both her safety and her comfort brought reassurance and a sense of being cherished. At last she had someone with whom she could be natural and, perhaps of even more importance, someone on whose devotion she had the first claim. Moreover she had not to share John Brown, unlike Albert, with her children and the nation. His time was exclusively hers.

John Brown, the Highland servant who helped to abate the grief of the widowed Queen: from a bust by Sir Edgar Boehm, 1869.

Victoria was always whole-hearted. When she gave her affection and trust she did so without stint, always refusing to listen to the slightest criticism of its recipient. So it was to be with John Brown, who came to play an increasingly important part in the Queen's life. At first he was merely the Queen's Highland servant, though from the beginning he took orders only from her, for which he came to her own room. He accompanied her on all occasions, sitting on the box of her carriage. Increasingly, the members of the royal household found themselves forced to communicate with the Queen through Brown. Both they and the Queen's children began to resent the way in which he was assuming the position of personal friend and confidant. The Prince of Wales disliked him cordially, Prince Alfred was engaged in a long quarrel, while between Brown and the rest of the household a persistent struggle existed. Had the Queen been taking her full part in the ceremonial duties of her office, her attachment to Brown might have remained a subject of Court gossip, but combined with her constant retreats to Balmoral or, when Parliament was sitting, to Osborne, public discontent seized on their relationship, which the cheaper Press blew up into a scandal. Just as once Victoria had been nicknamed 'Mrs Melbourne', now people spoke of 'Mrs Brown'. There were even rumours of a secret marriage, while some people suggested that John Brown was enjoying the Prince Consort's privileges without that ceremony. Her family and ministers grew extremely worried about the mounting tide of criticism that threatened to undermine the monarchy itself. Victoria refused to listen to criticism either of Brown or of the infrequency of her public appearance.

She had, in fact, started to come out of her almost unbroken seclusion during Disraeli's first premiership, to the extent of opening Parliament in person in 1867, and laying the foundation stone for Miss Nightingale's new hospital, St Thomas's, in 1868. She had, however, refused Gladstone's request that she should open Parliament in 1870, even though she made occasional public appearances in 1871 when she attended the opening of the Albert Hall and Blackfriars Bridge. These ordeals, she considered, should have been sufficient for any woman to face in her state of health, which she refused against all the evidence to believe had materially improved. Any suggestions that she might dispense with John Brown's services, or even use them in a less ostentatious manner, she dismissed with contempt. He was necessary to her comfort and her safety; even if he had not been, her own particular brand of obstinate loyalty would have made her stand by him to the end. In short she would appear in public when she felt able, and Brown would stay. Her family and ministers alike retreated defeated.

The result was that the Crown had never been so unpopular since the time when George IV had tried to divorce Queen Caroline. Even at the height of her earlier popularity, there had been attempts on Victoria's life. Only two of these had vague political motives, the others were the actions of unbalanced or inadequate individuals, who failed to load their guns properly or who aimed to threaten rather than to kill. The first took place in June 1840; in 1842 there were two such attempts,

THE OUTRAGE.

One of the attempts on the Queen's life which took place in the 1840s. This attempt, in May 1849, was made by John Hamilton, an out-of-work labourer from Ireland.

then a further one in 1849, while in the following year an un-hinged retired lieutenant of the 10th Hussars, called Pate, struck the Queen violently over the head with a stick. When she appeared at the Royal Opera House that night the audience rose and cheered her for five minutes, applauding her courage and giving vent to their relief at her escape. But by 1871 public enthusiasm had turned sour. Most people were ignorant of the hours which the Queen devoted to public business. The majority wanted some visible proof that they were getting value for money in return for a Civil List of £385,000. When, therefore, application was made to Parliament for an annuity for Prince Arthur on his twenty-first birthday, criticism was exacerbated. In September a pamphlet entitled *What Does She*

Do With It? appeared, and everywhere the working-class Press was making insinuations of private extravagance and public parsimony. The charges were both unjust and unfair. The royal income went further because, as a result of the Prince Consort's stewardship, the royal establishments were managed with economy, and in this connection it is worth noticing that both Osborne and Balmoral had been bought out of these savings. Such facts were either unknown or ignored. One form taken by this public dissatisfaction was a demand that if the Queen were indeed too ill to perform her public duties, then she should abdicate in favour of the Prince of Wales, who, with his lovely wife, went everywhere and was correspondingly popular. Some extremists were prepared to go still further and to dispense with the monarchy altogether. In 1870 there had been a rather ineffectual rally of republican supporters in Hyde Park, which nobody had taken seriously. It was a different matter when the Radical MP Sir Charles Dilke, in a public lecture given in Newcastle in November 1871, accused the Queen of neglecting her duty, of having enormous savings hoarded away, and argued the case for a republic. Victoria, who on this occasion had been genuinely ill during the summer at Balmoral, was hurt and distressed by the attack. She was also annoyed that Gladstone had not repudiated the charges against her with more vigour. His defence was interesting. In reply he argued that Dilke had overshot the mark and had in fact turned public opinion against him and that the wisest course was to damp down the whole issue by not feeding the fires of controversy. With regard to Dilke's attack on the royal finances, Gladstone further pointed out that if this were to be fully met, it would involve the discussion of matters that 'in the present state of the public mind' he thought unwise.

The autumn of 1871 was to see this nadir of royal unpopularity, followed by a sudden swift upsurge of sympathy, which completely destroyed the support which Dilke had enjoyed. On 22 November the Queen, who was at Balmoral, was told that the Prince of Wales had suffered a mild attack of typhoid. She at once sent Sir William Jenner to Sandringham, which was now the Prince's home, and herself returned to Windsor. By the 27th, the news was less reassuring and two days later she went to Sandringham, where she found her son rather better than she had feared. She therefore returned to Windsor on 1 December. Unfortunately the invalid then took a turn for the worse and the Queen, with her daughter Louise, hurried back to Norfolk. For some days the situation looked grim and both Leopold and Beatrice were summoned. Then came an agonising wait, as the anniversary of Prince Albert's death from the same disease drew near. Victoria seems to have been convinced that she would lose her son as she had lost her husband.

One of the saddest aspects of her early widowhood had been that she had not felt she could turn to her eldest son for support and consolation, because she blamed him for having been its very cause. By his immoral escapade he had broken her Angel's heart, and had caused Albert to travel up to Cambridge while suffering the early effects of typhoid. For a time she could hardly bear to see Bertie, though he, poor young man, was only too anxious to help and comfort his mother in any way he could. In time, her maternal instincts had enabled her to transfer his guilt to the lax behaviour of the fashionable world around him, but she continued to be influenced by the fear which had also haunted his father that, in spite of the care with which they had planned and supervised his education, Bertie had not developed those qualities of hard work and dedication which they valued so highly. She acknowledged him to be an affectionate, dutiful and amiable son, but continued to consider him too indiscreet and inexperienced to share her responsibilities as Queen. When, for instance, in 1864 the Prince asked to be allowed to see the foreign dispatches, all that his mother would concede was that he should be furnished with a *précis* of the more interesting ones, and given such information about the general policy of the government as the Queen thought desirable. Once again Victoria was not prepared to risk any opposition to her views; she argued that it was wiser that the Prince should not have unrestricted access to the essential information. In other ways, too, his mother thwarted her son's chances of playing much part in public life. When Disraeli pressed for the Prince to have a permanent residence of his own in Ireland, Victoria opposed it; when he wanted to attend the wedding of his wife's sister in Russia, he was accused of remaining so '*little* quiet at home and always running about'. Yet, when he remained at home the Queen gave him no responsibility and

'The country, and all of us would like to see you a little more stationary'

173

Max Beerbohm's satire on the uneasy relationship between the Queen and her eldest son and heir. This cartoon, entitled 'The rare, the rather awful visits of Albert Edward, Prince of Wales, to Windsor Castle' comes from Beerbohm's *Things Old and New*.

no training for his future position as King. Even when he was allowed to take his place beside her at an investiture, Victoria remembered with nostalgia that he was standing in his father's place.

Inevitably the Prince was driven back onto a life of pleasure. Instead of being grateful that her son was able to some extent to mitigate the consequences of her own seclusion by being much in the public eye, the Queen continued to try to supervise even these activities. She disliked the Prince's fondness for race meetings. In the June of 1870, before Ascot, Victoria wrote

174

advising him to confine his attendance to the two great days, Tuesday and Thursday, instead of attending all four meetings. Moreover, because any example set by him was important, she suggested that he should not encourage the sport by attending every year. It was in his own interests, Victoria pointed out, that Bertie should gather round him only good, steady and distinguished people. On this occasion her dutiful son did offer a mild remonstrance, pointing out that though there was much in the racing world of which he too disapproved, nevertheless racing was the national sport and there was more chance of improving its standards by attending the important meetings than by staying away. He then added a quiet rebuke, writing, 'as I am past twenty-eight and have some considerable knowledge of the world and society, you will I am sure, at least I trust, allow me to use my own discretion in matters of this kind'.

Victoria had a basic and not altogether unfounded distrust of the fashionable set in which the Prince was moving. In immediate Court circles she insisted on a complete observance of the Prince Consort's rigid moral code, and believed it her duty to prevent peerages being conferred on anyone, however great their abilities or services, whose moral character was open to question, a qualification which on occasions her ministers found inconvenient. Outside the Court, standards were changing. In the past birth had been the passport to social acceptance, with wealth a bad second. Now these attributes were being reversed. Wealth had always been important but it had taken two, sometimes three generations, before it had enabled a family to establish its position. Now the *nouveaux riches* were becoming increasingly accepted and with this, to some extent, came the brash display of new-found affluence. The laxity of the set frequented by the heir to the throne was dramatically demonstrated when one of its members, Sir Charles Mordaunt, brought a suit for divorce against his wife and *subpœnaed* the Prince of Wales, whose letters to Lady Mordaunt were read out in court. These were in fact quite innocuous, while Lady Mordaunt was herself clearly mentally unhinged, but the mere fact that the Prince of Wales could be called upon to give evidence in a divorce court was in itself a landmark of changing times. Though the Queen believed her son to be innocent of any misconduct, it was deeply disturbing to her that he should be associating with people whose conduct was so open to question. It was clear that mother and son viewed life from very different angles.

As he lay apparently at death's door, all this was forgotten; Victoria wrote 'one great anxiety seems to absorb everything else'. His illness had also come as a shock to the country as a whole; royalty still had an aura of romance and magic in a world where counter-attractions were few. When the Prince made what seemed an almost miraculous recovery, he and the Queen attended a great public service of thanksgiving at St Paul's on 27 February 1872. They received a thunderous welcome as they entered the City at Temple Bar, that marked the reconciliation between a frustrated people and a secluded Queen. When, two days later, Victoria was threatened with a pistol – which later proved to be unloaded – while driving out, the seal was set on this reconciliation, republicanism and criticism alike subsided, leaving Sir Charles Dilke a lone figure crying in the wilderness of a hostile House of Commons. The Queen was once again prepared to play her part in the life of the nation. From 1874 this was made easier by her accord with her Prime Minister, Benjamin Disraeli, in his second term of office.

With the death of Lord Palmerston, British politics entered a new phase. The older combinations in the struggle for political power now hardened into two well-organised parties. This was the culmination of a process that had been taking place ever since the Reform Act of 1832, and which, by increasing the number of urban voters, made it imperative to organise the electoral rolls in which they were registered. Both Russell and Palmerston had been Whigs of the old school, willing to ally with the middle classes in order to preserve aristocratic leadership and to protect property against the propertyless masses. They believed in constitutional, but not necessarily democratic, government. It was because current revolutionary movements in Europe were directed against autocratic rulers that Palmerston so often appeared to encourage them, and not because he was essentially a democrat. Meanwhile, Sir Robert Peel had been gradually laying the foundations for a new Conservative party to replace the old Tories, who were largely the country gentlemen. Unlike the Whigs, Peel looked forward rather than backwards but, unlike the

Radicals, placed greater emphasis on administrative reform than on further instalments of Parliamentary reform, as the best means of dealing with the needs of a changing society in a changing world. Accordingly his ministry, during the period 1842 to 1846, was responsible for much important legislation along these lines. This included a series of acts establishing Free Trade, a major reconstruction of the Bank of England, an important Factory Act, a consolidating Railway Act and, finally, the repeal of the Corn Laws. This split the party, with important consequences for the next twenty years. The Peelites,

THE DERBY, 1867. DIZZY WINS WITH "REFORM BILL."

MR. PUNCH. "DON'T BE TOO SURE; WAIT TILL HE'S *WEIGHED.*"

In 1866, Lord Russell hoped to pass a further measure of Parliamentary reform, but was blocked by lack of support from his own party. Disraeli, coming into power in 1866 with Lord Derby, decided to take 'a leap in the dark' and put through the Second Reform Act.

including Gladstone, tended to act with the Whigs, which left the Conservatives, under Lord Derby and his henchman Disraeli, too weak to provide a strong alternative government to that of Aberdeen, Russell and Palmerston.

After Lord Palmerston's death, Lord Russell, who was anxious to introduce some further measure of Parliamentary reform, found his position weakened still further because one wing of his supporters was strongly opposed to any such measure. Reluctantly the Queen, who was not personally opposed to further Parliamentary reform, but who did dislike ministerial crises, sent for Lord Derby and in 1866 he formed an administration with Disraeli as his Chancellor of the Exchequer. In 1868 ill-health forced Derby to resign and Disraeli became Prime Minister. Victoria was at last to have a Prime Minister with whom she was able to establish those close personal relations which were always so important to her and which, apart from the smooth transaction of public business, made her feel cherished and admired as a woman as well as a Queen. Disraeli's first letter to his sovereign sounded this new note. He could only, he wrote, offer his devotion while hoping that the Queen would 'deign not to withhold from him the benefit of your Majesty's guidance' in the great affairs of State. This was a most delightful change from those 'two dreadful old men', Russell and Palmerston; once again Victoria felt appreciated. Alas this happy interlude was all too brief. In spite of passing the Reform Act of 1867, which in general enfranchised the urban working-man, the Conservatives were

LEFT William Ewart Gladstone, the great Liberal Prime Minister, whom Victoria found so difficult to understand and to deal with. Photograph of about 1860.
RIGHT Benjamin Disraeli, Earl of Beaconsfield and Conservative Prime Minister. His relationship with the Queen, whom he nicknamed 'the Faery', was very close and sympathetic, and he filled the role which Lord Melbourne had played so many years earlier. Portrait by John Millais.

178

defeated in the general election in November. The Queen was forced to send for Mr Gladstone, while at the same time showing her appreciation of Mr Disraeli by creating his wife, odd little Mary-Anne, Viscountess Beaconsfield.

Victoria had always found Gladstone's quirks of conscience hard to understand while he, in turn, had little of Disraeli's sympathetic and intuitive knack of managing her. Instead of giving her a clear exposition of a situation or a problem, he muddled the Queen with long discourses, full of parentheses and suppositions which wearied without enlightening her. Though Victoria accepted the fact of his 'goodness', a quality which ought to have commended him to her, his incomprehensible behaviour often drove her to think him either mad or a humbug. It was no good base for a working partnership. Nevertheless, compared with his later ministries, Gladstone's first tenure of office, which lasted until 1874, was relatively smooth. The Queen accepted, though she disliked, his bill to disestablish the Irish Church, arguing shrewdly that it would do little to solve the increasingly difficult Irish problem. Officially she made her views clear by refusing to open Parliament in person and thus give tacit approval to Gladstone's measures, though her excuse was the state of her health. The major tussles between the Queen and her Prime Minister arose from his attempts to drag Victoria from her seclusion though for once her pleas of ill-health were genuine. She was wretchedly ill for most of the summer of 1871, and once convinced that this was so, Gladstone was all sympathy and concern. Nevertheless, it was with relief that the Queen was able to replace him by Disraeli in 1874.

For six years Victoria had a Prime Minister with whom she could work amicably, a minister who made her feel important and in whose company she could relax. It was almost like the old days with Melbourne, when ministerial visits became a pleasure and business was leavened with gossip and pleasant conversations. Much has been made of the romantic passages between them, a plump widow in her fifties and the elderly eccentric who christened her 'the Faery'. No doubt Disraeli both flattered her and regarded her with a certain wry amusement, but there was affection as well as flattery in his elaborate compliments. It was gratifying to have a Prime Minister who on kissing hands murmured 'I plight my troth to the kindest of *Mistresses*' and Victoria enjoyed it. But if such speeches had been mere flattery she was shrewd enough to have sensed the fact. She gave affection because she also received it. Disraeli enjoyed the company of women – the death of his wife while he had been in opposition had left him a lonely old man. Though he found 'the Faery' exhausting, it was not only ambition that made him serve her. She in turn used his loyalty and his affection to get what she could not have got from another Prime Minister. After Disraeli's death the Queen told Granville that he had been 'one of the kindest, truest and best friends and wisest counsellors she ever had'. Because he took care to assure her that it was her right to be thoroughly informed about public business and that her advice was important, she felt that once more she was able to exercise adequate control over policy. This assumption did not always make life easy for Disraeli.

One topic on which she felt strongly was the increase of ritualism in the Established Church. Religion was taken seriously in Victorian England, and for much of her reign doctrinal controversies flourished, in particular those connected with the Tractarian Movement, itself a reaction against the earlier Evangelical Movement of the late eighteenth and early nineteenth centuries. Victoria herself was a stout Protestant with uncomplicated views on theology and a middle-of-the-road approach to them. She once told Disraeli that in her opinion the extreme High Church party did as much harm to the Established Church as the Evangelicals. She took her duties as Supreme Governor seriously, giving careful attention to Church appointments and, where she could, pressing for men with broad liberal views. Victoria was surprisingly sympathetic to the Irish Roman Catholics on the grounds that, as Albert had pointed out, being in the majority in Ireland they could hardly be described as Dissenters. On the other hand, she was very suspicious of Roman Catholic converts and of the papal claims to appoint a hierarchy in Britain. The root of Victoria's abhorrence of the High Church party, with its insistence on ritual, frequent communion and use of the confessional, was that she believed them 'to be *Roman Catholics at heart, and very insincere* as to their professions of attachment to the Church'.

1 May 1876, Victoria was proclaimed Empress of India, by the Titles Bill which Disraeli passed through Parliament. This cartoon shows the Queen exchanging her British Crown for the imperial diadem.

"NEW CROWNS FOR OLD ONES!"

Accordingly she used Disraeli's devotion to her wishes to push through a Public Worship Act, to check excessive ritualistic practices in the Established Church. Because religious feeling was running high, this presented him with a most difficult task, but after much political manœuvring the bill became law in

The Oxford Movement

The Oxford Movement was a loose association of like-minded men from the University bent on reforming the slipshod ways of the Established Church. By 1837 the movement was in full swing and was circulating *Tracts for the Times* which were a constant source of controversy and discussion. The founders of the movement were John Keble, John Henry Newman and Hurrell Froude, who were soon joined by Edward Bouverie Pusey. The Queen looked upon the movement with great disfavour, and with their emphasis upon the value of symbolism as a reminder of eternal verities, she believed Pusey and Newman 'to be *Roman Catholics at heart and very insincere* as to their professions of attachment to the Church'.

RIGHT John Henry Newman, one of the founding members of the Oxford Movement. According to Dean Church it was 'Keble who inspired, Froude who gave the impetus and Newman who took up the work'. In 1845, however, Newman confirmed all the worst suspicions of the Queen and opponents of the Oxford Movement, by being received into the Roman Church. In 1879 he became a Cardinal. Portrait painted by Emmeline Deane in 1889, only a year before Newman's death.

LEFT Cartoon of 1858 showing the Bishop of London, Archibald Campbell Tait, reprimanding members of the High Church party for their desire to introduce candles and crucifixes into the Church.

RIGHT The Chapel of Keble College, designed by William Butterfield. John Keble died in 1866, and the college was founded as a memorial to him by public subscription in 1870. The College was built by William Butterfield, the great Victorian exponent of the Gothic revival.

A PROPER CHARGE.

B——P OF L—D—N. "YOU MUST NOT BRING YOUR PLAYTHINGS INTO CHURCH, MY LITTLE MEN."

LEFT Edward Bouverie Pusey, leader of the Oxford Movement, and a brilliant preacher. His sermon, the *Holy Eucharist, a comfort to the Penitent* made in 1843, so shocked the University authorities that he was suspended for two years from preaching. He also took part in every important theological controversy, endeavouring to find some form of basis for a union between the Churches of England and Rome. Watercolour by C. Pellegrini, 1875, drawn for *Vanity Fair*.

1874. The whole episode illustrates at once Victoria's own views, her pertinacity and her relations with Disraeli.

But of all Disraeli's services to her, the one which perhaps brought the Queen the most personal pleasure was when he managed to secure for her the title of Empress of India. Contrary to popular belief, this was the Queen's own ambition. Even before the Indian Mutiny, and still more when Lord Canning had become Viceroy, she had been interested in India. Moreover, the Queen wanted an Imperial title for personal reasons. There were now three Emperors in Europe, the Tsar, the Emperor of Austria and, since 1870, the Emperor of Germany, the father-in-law of her eldest daughter Vicky. If her daughter were one day to become an Empress, then so must 'Mama'. Public opinion was not enthusiastic. Indeed, Victoria was considerably annoyed by the difficulties that confronted Disraeli in his efforts to get the Titles Bill through Parliament. However, he succeeded and on 1 May 1876 Victoria was proclaimed Empress of India, with great ceremony at Delhi. Though strictly speaking Victoria was now an Empress in India and a Queen in Britain, she immediately imported an Indian flavour to her Court. There was a Durbar Room at Osborne, full of treasures from the East and, after the death of John Brown in 1883, she employed an Indian, Abdul Karim – the Munshi – as her personal servant. The airs which he gave himself brought him nearly as much unpopularity in Court circles as had been focussed on the late John Brown, which made the the Queen defend him with her usual tenacity. He was still in her service when she died. In desiring to become Empress of India Victoria displayed her usual combination of personal emotion and shrewd sense. She wanted to become an Empress but she also argued that the title would mean more in India than that of Queen of England. She was probably right.

If Victoria drove Disraeli to secure for her this coveted title, his purchase of the Khedive's shares in the Suez Canal was due to his own initiative. It was in some sense an indication that British public opinion was becoming more imperialistic. Even as late as 1865 Victoria had expected Canada to become independent, and thought that the most that could be hoped for was that it might accept one of her sons as its new ruler. Instead, in 1878, her daughter Louise with her husband, the

Marquess of Lorne, as the new Governor General went to Canada, which had been so restless during the early years of her reign, but now seemed content to remain a part of the Empire. The last four years of Disraeli's premiership saw a great outburst of what came to be known as 'jingoism', the occasion for which was the Russo-Turkish war of 1877. Revolts had broken out in the Turkish Balkan provinces in the suppression of which the Turks had used irregular troops, the Bashi-Bazouk, who had murdered thousands of Bulgarian peasants. During a year of European diplomacy, in 1876, the Great Powers had failed either to restrain Turkey or to force her to institute reforms, and Russia prepared to go to the help of the Christian Bulgarians. An ugly situation blew up which was to have considerable repercussions on both Victoria's public and private life. Turkey had been a British ally in the Crimean War and Victoria had an almost fanatical suspicion of Russia. She and Disraeli therefore minimised the Bulgarian atrocities, while Gladstone, who had recently gone into his first political retirement, re-emerged and stumped the country in a whirlwind campaign to turn the Turk out of Europe 'bag and baggage'. Whereupon the Queen, with her own brand of logic, managed to persuade herself that Gladstone and Russia had egged on the Turks to commit atrocities in order to force a war on Turkey! Behind the scenes the Queen worked furiously to create an anti-Russian front, so that for a time there seemed some danger that Britain herself might become involved. Luckily diplomacy prevailed and Beaconsfield – the title had been conferred on Disraeli in 1876 – covered himself with glory at the Congress of Vienna in 1878 where, in conjunction with Bismarck, he hammered out a solution for the Eastern Question. Meanwhile in the Music Halls they were singing:

> We don't want to fight but by jingo if we do
> We've got the ships, we've got the men,
> We've got the money too.

Other imperial adventures were less successful, at least in their early stages. The British determination to control Afghanistan, where Russian influence was feared, led to the murder of a British Mission in 1879, while an attempt to extend Natal against the Zulu King Cetewayo led to the appalling defeat at Isandhlwana. Moreover, the purchase of the Suez

'We don't want to fight but by jingo if we do We've got the ships, We've got the men, We've got the money too'

185

Glasallt Sheil, the small house at the end of Loch Muich, which the Queen had built about two miles from Balmoral. She would retire to it with one attendant and Princess Beatrice, when she wanted to get away from the formal life of the Court and the Household.

Canal shares involved Britain in the politics of Egypt, where the Khedive had gone bankrupt. In the Transvaal the Boers were threatening trouble. Though Cetewayo was ultimately defeated and Khandahar in Afghanistan recaptured, Gladstone was once again campaigning against a policy which he denounced as aggressive and extravagant, and when it was decided to hold a general election in March 1880 the Conservatives were defeated. To her intense dismay, the Queen was again faced with the loss of a minister who was also her friend, and with the constitutional necessity of countenancing policies that conflicted with her personal judgment. Two years later Beaconsfield died. Never again was Victoria to feel towards her Prime Minister as she had towards Disraeli.

Between them, the Scot and the Jew had pulled Victoria out of the slough of despair and restored to her the desire to live and a zest for life. Her journal, always a mirror of her emotions, displays a new lightness of heart, an enjoyment of little things, such as painting the view from her window, and the end of the old shrinking from publicity and crowds. She was happy to drive in an open landau from Paddington Station to Marlborough House to attend a garden party given by the Prince and Princess of Wales. When she and the Princess were at Osborne in the August of 1877, they went out in a barge to inspect the new ironclad, HMS *Thunderer*. Victoria was delighted to find that she had not lost her 'sea legs', though she found crawling into the gun turrets awkward and unpleasant. She even began to dance again, which she had not done for eighteen years, and found that, partnered by her son Arthur at an impromptu dance on Beatrice's birthday, she could do it as well as ever. One of the first indications that she was beginning to live her own life again, instead of existing on memories, was her building of a small house at the end of Loch Muich, near Balmoral, the Glasallt Sheil, or 'the Queen's House', where she could live a cosy, private life of her own, unhaunted by the past.

Even so, there were shadows, chiefly the shadow of death, as well as the sunshine of happier hours in these years. Lady Augusta Stanley who, as Lady Augusta Bruce, had been one of Victoria's household and a most trusted friend before her marriage to Dean Stanley, died in March 1876. Two years later Victoria's own daughter Alice – who, like Lady Augusta, had comforted and supported the Queen in her agony at Albert's death – by an odd quirk of fate, died on the anniversary of her father's death after nursing her children through diphtheria. Then, in March 1879, a grandson, one of Vicky's sons, died. He, like Prince Leopold, had suffered from haemophilia. Nevertheless, in spite of these family losses, Victoria found much happiness during the years. At last she had come to think better of 'dear Bertie' and had always been attached to his wife, Alexandra. Then in 1879 her son Arthur, whom Victoria always thought the most like Albert, married Princess Louise of Prussia. Unlike Alice's funereal wedding in 1861, Arthur's was celebrated with magnificence, despite Alice's recent death. The Queen wore the Koh-i-Noor diamond and a dress with a train. Court life was back to normal and Britain again had a visible Queen.

8
Victoria Triumphant: High Noon and Sunset 1879-1901

POLITICS BELONG to the history of the nation, but because Victoria's relations with her ministers was one of the most important ingredients in her happiness, or otherwise, politics are as much a part of her private as of her public life. Until his final retirement in 1893, Gladstone remained a major source of irritation and even distress. In comparison, Victoria's feelings towards her other Liberal Prime Minister, Lord Rosebery, were friendly; as a man she liked him, though they did not really agree on policy. When the Conservative leader, Lord Salisbury, had a majority in the Commons, ministerial business went smoothly, largely because there was no clash of any significance on questions of policy. For many years Victoria regarded Salisbury, with something less than strict constitutional propriety, as her main ally against Gladstone. But between him and the Queen there was none of the personal warmth that made public life so delightful in Disraeli's day.

After Disraeli's resignation Victoria had doubled and twisted like a hunted hare to avoid having Gladstone as her Prime Minister. At first she had refused to entertain the idea that anything so distasteful could be forced on her. Gladstone was not officially leader of the Liberal party, having earlier resigned in favour of Lord Granville, and the Queen had made it abundantly clear that after his despicable behaviour during the Russo-Turkish war she would never consent to his holding office again. When Granville and Hartington told her that only Gladstone could command a majority in the Commons, the Queen said bluntly that she could not give him her confidence and talked darkly of abdicating. In the end Victoria had to give way, but it was not an auspicious beginning. Indeed, she was always reporting hopefully on how ill he looked, and listened gleefully to accounts of splits within the Cabinet, where Radicals under Joseph Chamberlain fought right-wing Liberals such as the Duke of Argyll. At times the Queen's conduct hardly conformed to the constitutional convention that she must be above Party. Gladstone, understandably in the circumstances, told her as little of Cabinet business as he could, and she retaliated by using secret channels of information. She also corresponded privately with the leaders of the Opposition. In the case of Disraeli, Victoria was repeating only what she had done after Lord Melbourne's resignation and, whatever the

PREVIOUS PAGES Street decorations for Queen Victoria's Golden Jubilee, 1887.

190

world might think, she considered such letters justified on the grounds of personal friendship. Neither Melbourne then nor Disraeli now could bring themselves to discourage her: in their own ways they both loved the Queen. But in 1886 Victoria went even further. She began to supply Salisbury with inside information on Government business, in the hope of facilitating the fall of the obnoxious Gladstone. Her personal justification in so doing was her conviction that the good of the country required his removal from office, but in so doing she had departed far from the path laid down by Albert and Stockmar for a constitutional monarch.

In discussing her differences of opinion with Gladstone, it is easier to summarise these over his three ministries – that from 1880–5, that from the February to the July of 1886, and lastly from 1892 to his final retirement in the next year – than to attempt any strictly chronological treatment. Probably the issue on which the Queen felt most deeply was foreign policy, with which she had been intimately connected for fifty years.

In 1880, Gladstone succeeded Disraeli as Prime Minister and found that he had inherited several imperial problems from his predecessor, including Afghanistan, the Transvaal, Egypt and the Sudan.

LABOUR AND REST.

Ex-Head Gardener (*retired from business*). "WELL, WILLIAM, YER DON'T SEEM TO BE MAKIN' MUCH PROGRESS—*DO* YER!"
New Head Gardener. "WHY NO, BENJAMIN; YOU LEFT THE PLACE IN SUCH A PRECIOUS MESS!!"

Both she and Disraeli had a fondness for magnificent ideas and were stimulated by visions of empire. Gladstone's reactions were totally different. His approach to foreign affairs was basically moralistic, in the sense that he considered aggression morally wrong. Moreover imperial policies to a man who had made his reputation as a Chancellor of the Exchequer, seemed to involve unnecessary expenditure. When he succeeded Disraeli in 1880, several difficult imperial questions were pending. The murder of the British Mission in Afghanistan had been successfully avenged by Sir Frederick Roberts's capture of Khandahar. Gladstone not only decided that this should be given back, he also annoyed the Queen considerably by committing her to this in her speech opening Parliament, without first having obtained her approval. In Africa the Transvaal Boers, who had trekked from Cape Colony to found a new Afrikaander community beyond the Vaal River, once the Zulus had been defeated, proclaimed a republic in 1880. Next year, a small British force was defeated at Majuba Hill. In subsequent negotiations the British withdrew their claims to any part of the Transvaal, retaining only a vague suzereinty over its foreign relations. The Queen disapproved violently, and declared herself to be utterly disgusted and disheartened when her views were ignored.

The bitterest clash with Gladstone arose over the affairs of Egypt, a country in which, since the purchase of the Suez Canal shares, Britain held a vital interest. A revolt by a religious leader, Arabi, against the weak government of the Khedive led to the dispatch of British troops, Gladstone having decided that in this case intervention was justified. To Victoria's intense pride her son, Arthur of Connaught, commanded a battalion of the Guards at the victory of Tel-el-Kebir. The British government next felt forced to undertake the responsibility for the supervision of the Egyptian administration. This in turn involved an entanglement with the Sudan, which was controlled by Egypt. In 1883 a fanatical religious leader, the Mahdi, arose and almost wiped out the Egyptian army which was commanded by a British officer in Egyptian pay, Hicks Pasha. Victoria argued in favour of swift vigorous action but her ministers opposed. Instead, the Cabinet decided to evacuate the scattered garrisons still remaining in the Sudan. The choice of the man to do this was unfortunate: Colonel Charles Gordon, though a brilliant soldier, was the last man to be entrusted with the management of such a withdrawal. Once settled in Khartoum, he delayed and began to ask for reinforcements. Both criticism and defence of Gordon's actions lie outside the scope of a life of Queen Victoria, except insofar as she was a violent partisan. Again and again she urged that additional troops should be sent before it was too late. The Queen's urgency was justified. Khartoum fell on 25 January 1885, just as the relieving column, sent at last, was nearing the town. Victoria was so utterly disgusted with Gladstone's delay that she telegraphed 'en clair', instead of in the customary cypher, that 'to think that all of this might have been prevented and many precious lives saved by earlier action is too frightful'. In reply Gladstone tried to administer a sharp remonstrance to his sovereign for her unconstitutional revelation of her personal opinion, but both the votes in Parliament and the general election that followed made it clear that the public, like the Queen, blamed Gladstone for Gordon's death.

The third bone of contention between the Queen and her Prime Minister was Ireland. Gladstone was convinced that it was his mission to 'pacify Ireland', and it was this mission which both in 1880 and in 1892 drove him out of his retirement. This tremendous problem was not one in which the Queen, left to herself, would have felt a deep personal interest. Victoria did not understand the Irish and was inclined not to like them. For this Melbourne, with his half-humorous denigration of Irish grievances, was partly to blame. Momentarily this early impression had been destroyed by the miseries of the Irish famine, but with Peel's death there was no one sympathetic to Ireland whom she trusted who could explain to her the deep-seated nature of the Irish problem. In addition, the majority of the people with whom the Queen came into contact were Anglo-Irish landowners and as such unlikely to be impartial. As a result, Victoria gradually came to believe that the Irish disturbances were the work of agitators whose machinations had to be suppressed by stern measures in the interests of law and order. She was not anti-Irish insofar as she did not oppose Gladstone's policy for the disestablishment of the Irish Church, though she did not believe that it would have a significant

'To think that all of this might have been prevented and many precious lives saved by earlier action is too frightful'

OVERLEAF Pages from the 1897 Jubilee edition of *The Illustrated News*. RIGHT Portraits of the Queen at different times in her life, and of her eldest children, the Prince of Wales and the Empress Frederick, with their consorts and children. LEFT The development of transport during Victoria's reign, with portraits of pioneers in this field.

193

*'The union
of the Empire
is in danger
of disintegration'*

effect on Irish public opinion, nor did she oppose the principle of the Land Act with its emphasis on fair rents and fixity of tenure. But she did believe that there should first be a Coercion Act to restore order. She was shocked by the murders and crime in Ireland and felt that Gladstone pandered to lawlessness instead of dealing with it firmly. Later, his Home Rule programme seemed to the Queen to threaten the very existence of the Empire, whose guardian she had come to see herself. In May 1886 she told Gladstone that though she always *'wishes to be able* to give her Prime Minister her *full support'* she could not do so 'when the union of the Empire is in danger of disintegration'. Accordingly, in a most unconstitutional manner, she threw her influence into the defeat of Home Rule and rejoiced in its rejection. Knowing very little about Ireland – the Queen only visited it twice, in 1861 and 1900 – she never had that close sense of personal involvement which seemed to be necessary to waken her sympathies. Indeed, she constantly compared the loyalty of Scotland with the disloyalty of Ireland without ever grasping the completely different situations in the two countries. So to her dislike of Gladstone was added her incomprehension of the problem which he was dedicated to solve. That her opinion changed the issue in any way is unlikely. Once again it was an issue on which the Queen and the majority of her subjects agreed, namely that the Irish were a disorderly people who would never be satisfied with the solid measures of amelioration provided by Parliament, and that they must not be allowed to disrupt the Empire.

Victoria not only disliked Gladstone's Irish and Little Englander policies, she also disliked his Radical allies, men like Joseph Chamberlain with their democratic, almost republican, theories. This did not mean that Victoria was indifferent to social misery. Indeed the reverse was true. Here Melbourne's social conservatism, with its disregard for the long hours worked by factory children and for the demand for popular education, had been swamped by Albert's keen interest in housing and social reform. As a girl, Victoria had been easily touched by individual unhappiness or hardship, as a Queen she broadened her sympathies to groups and classes. Instinctively she was prepared to think well of the mass of the people, partly because she disliked the fashionable London set, who stood for all of which she most disapproved, loose morals, gambling, racing and, above all, idleness. These were the people whom Victoria blamed for all that she disliked in her own sons, particularly Bertie. Her own standards had more in common with the middle classes, but she was conscious of her responsibility to all her subjects and would have preferred to have gathered something like a classless society under her wing. Of Dickens she wrote that he felt that the future would see a much greater union of classes, adding 'I pray earnestly it may'. Where she could, the Queen encouraged those people and societies who were struggling to make life more tolerable for the poorer subjects. She was interested in housing which, for most of the urban working class was cramped, overcrowded and lacking sanitation though this last defect they shared with their betters for most of her reign. If the town of Windsor had not been full of open stinking ditches, the Prince Consort might never have contracted typhoid.

In 1866 Victoria herself suggested that she should write to Mr Peabody to thank him for his magnificent charity in giving £100,000 to a trust for improving housing for London's poor because, as he was an American citizen, she could not bestow on him any of the usual marks of distinction. Later, having read *The Bitter Cry of Outcast London*, based on an enquiry into the slums, she did her best to prod Gladstone into taking steps to improve housing. Other forces were working in the same direction – an article by Lord Salisbury even appeared in the *National Review* – by the end of 1833 'slumming' had become fashionable, and in 1884 a Royal Commission on Housing was appointed. In the same year the Queen conferred a knighthood upon Edwin Chadwick, an honour long overdue, for the pioneer work he had undertaken in the fight for better urban sanitation and housing for the labouring population. The Crimean War had first interested Victoria in hospitals: she laid the foundation stone for St Thomas's in 1868, while in 1876 she not only opened the new wing of the London Hospital, but afterwards toured the wards. Nor was her compassion confined to the sick: after reading a book on female prison life, Victoria made a personal visit to Parkhurst: she even inspected the Windsor workhouse. Nevertheless, there were strict limits to her benevolence. In accordance with the old adage that

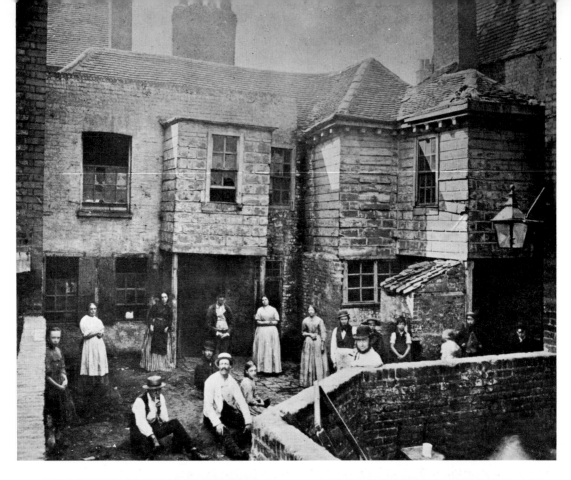

people who touch pitch become defiled, she frowned on those societies concerned with helping prostitutes, and even withheld her approval from the Salvation Army. Her sympathy was reserved for the deserving poor, except for a surprising tolerance, possibly induced by John Brown, for the man who took a drop too much.

In many ways Victoria was decidedly liberal in her views. She was in favour of giving the vote to respectable working men. She was definitely a supporter of what Gilbert called 'that annual blister, marriage with deceased wife's sister'. She was surprisingly tolerant towards Roman Catholics as long as they were not converts. She was utterly free of any trace of racial discrimination; black, brown and white, her subjects were all equal in her eyes. Even when she was refusing to take any part in public functions, Victoria received the Maori chiefs from New Zealand. After the submission of Cetewayo she received him too. In 1886, she was extremely interested in the great Colonial and Indian Exhibition, which she opened in person in May. In July she received representatives of all the nations connected with it, commenting with genuine interest on their appearance, from the Kaffir with only a blanket draped over him, to the little Bushmen who played on their pipes 'very funnily'. One of her objections to granting independence to the Boers was her conviction that they would be harsh towards the native population. Although so modern in some views, in others she was just as conservative. She had no patience with 'women's rights' and was horrified at the mere idea of women doctors. There was less inconsistency in this than might appear at first sight. In spite of her insistence on playing an active role in the government of the country, Victoria never really enjoyed the world of politics. Whatever her sphere of action, she could never have borne to be ignored, but it was in being a wife, and later a mother, that she found her deepest satisfactions.

A family of nine, all of whom married and produced children, gave her plenty of scope. Victoria was the complete matriarch: she loved her children but, undeterred by the memory of her own restricted childhood, she tried to control every detail of their lives. She was, as grandmothers often are, much more tolerant towards her grandchildren, who seemed to hold 'Gangan' in considerably less awe than did her own sons

The Queen became very interested in the problems of housing London's poor, and did her best to prod Gladstone into taking action to make improvements. LEFT This photograph shows Market Court in Kensington in about 1868. This is typical of innumerable courts in mid-Victorian cities, gloomy, filthy and insanitary.
BELOW LEFT Gustave Doré came to London in the mid-nineteenth century and portrayed the terrible overcrowded squalor of its poorer inhabitants in his nightmarish engravings. This illustration of London in 1872 comes from *The London Pilgrimage.*

The Salvation Army

The Salvation Army was founded in 1878 by General Booth to fight intemperance, prostitution and exploitation of the working classes. The Queen did not entirely approve of the activities of Booth and his colleagues, as she felt that they should confine their help to the 'deserving poor'.

RIGHT General William Booth, who was originally a regular preacher of the Methodist New Connection, but broke loose and began his career as an independent revivalist. In 1864 he went to London and founded at Whitechapel the Christian Mission which became the Salvation Army. Booth modelled its orders and regulations on those of the British Army, making himself 'General'. In 1890 he published *In Darkest England, and the Way Out*, his scheme to remedy pauperism and vice by various expedients. By the end of the century his ideas were no longer ridiculed and the active encouragement of the Prince of Wales helped his cause to gain public recognition.

LEFT Engraving of 1882 showing the various activities of the Salvation Army, including an afternoon meeting in the Grecian Theatre, and General William Booth with his wife Catherine Mumford, who did so much to help the movement.

RIGHT The social campaign of the Salvation Army, which grew to become a well-organised agency for relief and rehabilitation. Pauperism and vice were to be reduced by establishing colonies where the destitute could be given useful work, by the reclamation of prostitutes and the helping of discharged prisoners, and the provision of legal aid for the poor. Coloured engraving from Booth's *In Darkest England*.

and daughters. Victorian conventions were on her side. Respect and obedience to parental wishes was expected and family discipline was strict. Her grown-up sons, summoned suddenly into their mother's presence, apologised almost sheepishly for appearing in smoking jackets – smoking being a frowned-upon indulgence to be confined to the smoking room, which at Balmoral had to be vacated by midnight for the convenience of the servants! Her sons had always been something of a problem. Apart from Bertie, Victoria had been shocked to learn that Affie had been involved in an affaire while on naval duty at Malta; Leopold was often difficult, because his haemophilia so frustrated his longing for an active life, and because he found his mother's protective care stifling; only Arthur seemed completely satisfactory. Her daughters were less of a problem, apart from the need to arrange suitable marriages for them. Only Vicky, the Princess Royal, had been married before her father's death, though Alice was already engaged to Prince Louis of Hesse, whom she married soon after. Victoria tried to keep the young couple with her as long as possible for her own convenience. As she wrote to Leopold 'A married daughter I MUST have living with me.' She then proceeded, with a wonderfully unconscious self-centredness, to unfold her plan to keep the Princess Helena, known in the family as Lenchen, with her until she was nineteen or twenty, and then to look out for 'a young sensible prince' for her daughter to marry. The idea was then for them to make their home with the Queen during her whole lifetime because, as she confessed 'Lenchen is so useful, and her whole character so well adapted to live in the house that I could not give her up.' The only requisite for Helena's husband was plenty of good sense and high moral worth, combined with a sufficient income to enable them to live independently after the Queen's death! In 1866 Victoria found her a husband in Prince Christian of Schleswig-Holstein. Princess Louise, the next daughter, did not marry until she was twenty-two, not because of any restriction by the Queen, but because she had shown no inclination to do so until she fell in love with the heir to the Duke of Argyll, Lord Lorne. She was the first of Victoria's children to marry a subject. The Queen's explanation of this to the Prince of Wales, whom she thought might not welcome the idea, showed her at her shrewdest and most realistic. Marriages to German princes, she argued, were always unpopular with the British; foreign alliances could split the families when their dynastic ambitions conflicted, as for instance when Prussia, where Vicky's husband was Crown Prince, invaded Alice's husband's principality of Hesse-Darmstadt. Moreover, marriage to a subject would not only avoid these difficulties, it would 'strengthen the Throne *morally* as well as physically'.

Victoria was equally anxious that her sons should make satisfactory marriages, although they all took foreign wives. She was very fond of her eldest daughter-in-law, Alex of Denmark, even though she was sometimes exasperated by her adoption of modern manners, of which the Queen disapproved. Her second son, Alfred, who was destined to succeed his childless uncle, Ernest of Coburg, married Marie, the only daughter of the Tsar of Russia, in 1873. The Queen did not like the connexion; her distrust of Russia was too deep-seated, and the fact that her son was marrying into an Imperial house probably did something to sharpen the Queen's own ambition to be an Empress. Later she became reconciled to the marriage and grew fond of her new daughter-in-law whom she described as having a friendly manner and a pleasant face, admitting that 'there is something very fresh and attractive about her'. Victoria was also pleased to discover that her new daughter spoke English wonderfully well. Another matrimonial hurdle had been successfully negotiated. In 1878 Prince Arthur told his mother that he wanted to marry Princess Louise Margaret of Prussia, with whom he had fallen in love. Again Victoria was not enthusiastic. She did not like Louise's parents, whose own marriage had broken down, and tried to persuade Arthur at least to look elsewhere first. But, on her favourite son looking 'so sad and earnest, yet so dear and gentle', her mother's heart was softened, especially as she had to admit hearing nothing but good of his prospective bride. The marriage took place in 1879. The problem of finding a suitable bride for Prince Leopold, who was anxious to marry, was complicated by his poor health. In 1880, however, he met and liked the Princess Helen of Waldeck. Next year he proposed and was accepted, and they were married in 1882. The Queen was saddened to see the bridegroom 'still lame and shakey', but she was reported as

being in excellent spirits, wearing her widow's weeds with long gauze streamers, on her head a glittering tiara and the small crown Imperial, and on her bosom the broad ribbon of the Garter and the great Koh-i-noor diamond.

The last to go was the baby of the family, Princess Beatrice, in some ways the closest to her mother of all Victoria's daughters. She had been only four when her father died, and in the sad years that followed was her mother's constant companion. It was she who christened Victoria's widow's cap 'her sad cap', and had done something to cheer her with her own gay and sometimes naughty ways. It was a great shock to Victoria when Beatrice fell in love with the handsome Prince Henry of Battenberg. Beatrice met him at the marriage of his brother Louis to Princess Victoria of Hesse in 1884. The mere idea of losing her last unmarried daughter came as a great blow. For a time she refused to face the possibility, but finally gave her consent on condition that Beatrice and her husband, nicknamed 'Liko' in the royal family, lived with the Queen. As Victoria explained to the Duke of Grafton 'it would have been *quite out of the question* for her ever to have left the Queen; and *she* would *never* have *wished* it herself, knowing well how impossible it was for her to leave her mother'. To modern ears

ABOVE LEFT Queen Victoria at Coburg in April 1894, during a visit to her eldest daughter, the Empress Frederick of Prussia. Left to right, Arthur, Duke of Connaught, Alfred, Duke of Edinburgh, Queen Victoria, her eldest grandson, the Kaiser William II, the Empress Frederick and Edward, Prince of Wales.

ABOVE In July 1885,
Victoria's youngest child,
Princess Beatrice, was
married to Prince Henry
of Battenberg. The Queen
gave her consent on
condition that the young
couple should live with her.

such demanding possessiveness has an unpleasant ring; in extenuation of Victoria's selfishness, it must be remembered that Victorian daughters were expected to sacrifice their own happiness to that of their parents. To contemporaries the Queen's attitude would not have seemed unreasonable. The marriage took place at Whippingham parish church near Osborne, the first royal marriage – apart from Princess Alice's nuptials – not to be treated as a great occasion. Victoria however declared 'that a happier looking couple could rarely be seen kneeling at the altar together'. In every way it was a most successful marriage. In the words of the old adage, the Queen had not lost a daughter but gained a son, though the time was to come when Liko found the claustrophobic atmosphere of the family and Court routine so stifling that he longed to get away from it to return to the active life of a soldier.

With so many marriages and the nineteenth-century attitude towards child-bearing, the royal nurseries filled rapidly. Victoria had twenty-nine grandchildren who survived infancy, and in all of them she took a deep interest. The first of these was Vicky's son William, later the Kaiser William II of the First World War. As her eldest grandson, he always held a special place in Victoria's affections, though he was a difficult child and often annoyed her by the way he gave himself airs. Later, after he became Kaiser, he adopted anti-British policies, which she resented as Queen. Nevertheless a deep personal affection bound William to his grandmother, and at the end of her life he rushed to his 'beloved Grandmama's' bedside, and was beside her when she died. After the birth of two more children to Vicky, the Princess of Wales bore two sons in quick succession: Albert Victor, known in the family as Eddy, born in 1864, and George, later George V, in 1865. From the beginning, the Queen took the greatest interest in the Wales boys. She used to have them to stay with her and later, when they went to sea as naval cadets in the *Britannia*, she showed an anxious concern for their well-being. They returned her affection: though, as Sir Frederick Ponsonby's *Memoirs* show, the Queen could be a dragon to her household in her old age, at Osborne in the family circle she was often a gay old lady, very happy at a dance at Balmoral in 1890 to dance a quadrille with Eddy.

As soon as her grandchildren became of marriageable age,

Four generations of British monarchy: Queen Victoria with her eldest son, Edward, Prince of Wales (later Edward VII), her grandson, George (later George V) and his eldest son, Prince Edward of York (later Edward VIII).

PREVIOUS PAGES The Queen arriving in an open carriage outside St Paul's Cathedral on 22 June 1897 to attend a service of thanksgiving at her Diamond Jubilee. Painting by Andrew Gow.

the Queen took an intense interest in the selection of suitable partners for them and the ramifications of her family quickly spread even further over Europe as her grandchildren presented her with great-grandchildren. One of these Alice, the daughter of Victoria of Hesse who had married Louis of Battenberg, in her turn married Andrew of Greece, whose son, Prince Philip, married yet another great-great-granddaughter of Queen Victoria, the present Queen Elizabeth II. Other children that sprang from the marriage of Victoria of Hesse were Louise, who married the King of Sweden, and Louis, the present Earl Mountbatten of Burma. Victoria's younger sister, Alix, married the ill-fated Tsar Nicholas II of Russia and perished with him in 1918, during the Russian Revolution. But the marriage that concerned Queen Victoria most closely was that of her grandson Eddy, who was expected some day to succeed his father as King of England. She was delighted when, in 1891, Eddy told her that he was going to marry May, the young niece of the Queen's cousin George, Duke of Cambridge. May Teck – her mother Mary had married Francis of Teck – was 'so suitable'. Victoria's judgment was not at fault: as Queen Mary, young May did indeed fill her royal role most admirably, though not as the wife of Eddy, who died suddenly of pneumonia shortly before his wedding day, but as the consort of his brother, later George v.

Eddy's death was not the first to shatter the family circle and bring grief to the Queen. Alice was already dead, and her death was followed in 1884 by that of Prince Leopold. Though in some ways his health had made him the most difficult of her children, this fact had made him especially dear, to her. 'I am a poor desolate old woman, and my cup of sorrow overflows', she mourned in her journal, praying 'Oh! God in his mercy, spare my other dear children.' The next to be snatched away was the Queen's beloved son-in-law, Vicky's husband Fritz. He had been dying of cancer of the throat when he succeeded his father as Emperor of Germany, and lived to reign only ninety-nine days. Victoria had loved Fritz for himself and grieved for her daughter, telegraphing to her grandson, now Kaiser William ii, that she was broken-hearted. In 1892 came the news of the death of another son-in-law, Louis of Hesse, in the very same year as the heartbreak of young Eddy's death. A final blow came in 1895 when Beatrice's husband, Prince Henry of Battenberg, longing for a more active life, wrung from the Queen permission to join a military expedition against the Ashanti, who were constantly slave-raiding on the Gold Coast. He never even got to the front. He developed fever and died while being brought home. Princess Beatrice survived him until 1944, the last of Queen Victoria's children to live into the new world. The Queen was spared the news of her eldest daughter's death, which occurred shortly after Victoria's own in 1901, but she knew that Vicky was desperately ill and must have realised that she was unlikely to recover. During the last years of Victoria's life death seemed to hover perpetually. It was the penalty of marrying young and living to old age.

Nevertheless, though she was widowed so soon, and though as a mother Victoria had her fair share of maternal anxieties, her role both as a wife and as a mother brought her great happiness, more than falls to the lot of many women.

As a Queen, her life ended on a triumphal note. The sad years of seclusion, when the *Times* fulminated against her neglect of public duty and the republicans seemed to be an ever-increasing danger, were not only long over but long forgotten. Victoria had become an institution. From the 1880s, her public appearances were numerous and wherever she went on State occasions, such as the opening of Parliament, or when she merely drove from the station to Buckingham Palace, she was greeted by friendly crowds. The little old lady had become a cherished mascot of the London scene. Even her subjects in the provinces were given occasional opportunities to see their Queen, as they had been in the days when Victoria had her husband to support her. In 1861 she had visited Liverpool with him, now in 1886 she returned there to open 'An International Exhibition of Navigation and Commerce'. For once, the sun failed her and instead of the proverbial 'Queen's weather' she was greeted with wind and rain. Nothing daunted, the royal party armed with waterproofs and umbrellas drove in an open landau. All the streets were gaily decorated, and even the rain, which fell steadily, appeared unable to damp the enormous enthusiasm of the crowds. Both this exhibition and the Colonial and Indian Exhibition were, however, but preludes to the celebration of the Queen's Golden Jubilee which was to mark the fiftieth year of her reign.

It was celebrated with great pomp, as befitted so great an occasion. On 20 June, accompanied by Princess Beatrice and 'Liko', the Queen drove through gaily-decorated streets from the Castle to Windsor station, then from Paddington in an open landau to Buckingham Palace, greeted everywhere by enormous crowds of cheering people. Waiting to greet her in the picture gallery was a large gathering of kings and princes, her invited guests. This was followed by an enormous luncheon party and in the evening a large dinner party in the Supper Room, a very splendid affair. The company sat around a horseshoe-shaped table, the men resplendent in uniform, the women elegantly dressed, while in the background the buffet was covered with gold plate. Next day came the magnificence of the procession to the service of thanksgiving at Westminster.

A contemporary account describes how 'The Queen's face was tremulous with emotion, and yet there was triumph as well as grateful courtesy in her bearing, as she bowed her acknowledgments to her subjects.' In the carriage with the Queen were the Princess of Wales and the German Crown Princess, the latter described as 'beaming with delight and happiness to find that her countrymen still held her dear'. One of the greatest ovations was reserved for Vicky's husband Fritz who, the description continued, 'sat his charger as proudly as a medieval knight' and whose 'fair, frank face became radiant with delight' at the applause he received. After the ceremony the Queen returned to the Palace amid the 'passionate demonstrations of loyalty'. All London was *en fête* with fireworks and illuminations, while at the Palace Victoria had to face another luncheon and dinner party, followed by further presentations in the Ball Room. No wonder, as she confessed, she was half-dead with fatigue. No wonder, too, that she wrote in her journal that 'this never-to-be-forgotten day will always leave the most gratifying and heart-stirring memories behind'. As she sat enthroned in Westminster Abbey, she thought how proud Albert would have been, could he have sat beside her then. Yet exhausted as Victoria must have been, next day she still found the energy to grace a monster gathering of some twenty-seven thousand school-children, who were being given a Jubilee party in Hyde Park. Indeed for the rest of the month the Queen's public engagements followed hard and fast.

Ten years later, the Queen celebrated her Diamond Jubilee. By then sorrow and age had sapped her energies. This time Victoria had to receive her guests in a wheel-chair, while telegrams poured in too fast to be opened. The next day once again was a day of processions and thanksgiving, but in deference to the Queen's age, the latter was confined to a short service outside St Paul's. Once again she was greeted with the usual cheering crowds, as she drove there in her landau drawn by eight cream horses. At her Jubilee in 1887 all the crowned heads of Europe, most of them her relations, had gathered to greet her and had ridden in her procession. The Diamond Jubilee was a family gathering with a difference. It was the gathering of her larger family, whose representatives were not crowned heads but colonial premiers, come to give thanks with

'This never-to-be forgotten day will always leave the most gratifying and heart-stirring memories behind'

The Diamond Jubilee, 1897

At the celebrations for the Queen's Golden Jubilee, crowned heads from Europe had come to England to greet her, but at the Diamond Jubilee, celebrations ten years later, she was joined by representatives from every part of the Empire.

Troops from the colonies marched in the processions and demonstrated to the people of England their Empire on which 'the sun would never set'.

LEFT The Durbar Room at Osborne, which was created for Victoria after she became Empress of India. It now contains many of her Jubilee gifts presented to the Queen by her Imperial guests in 1897.

ABOVE The Queensland
Mounted Rifles in
the Diamond Jubilee
procession on 22 June 1897.
LEFT Jubilee souvenir
plate made to
commemorate the longest
reign on record. This plate
is typical of the kind of
mementoes made
at the time.

their Empress-Queen. It was a symbol of this new world that, before leaving Buckingham Palace, the Queen pressed an electric button which telegraphed a message throughout the Empire, 'From my heart I thank my beloved people. May God bless them', and so provided a precedent for the royal broadcast on Christmas Day that still links the Commonwealth. This again was another 'never to be forgotten day'. Though she was very weary, Victoria, like the gallant old trooper that she was, carried on to its end.

The last four years of her reign were lived in increasing shadows. Most of her old friends were already dead. Lady Augusta, Lady Ely, Lady Churchill, her devoted secretary Henry Ponsonby – he died in 1895 – Dean Stanley, all were gone, together with a host of other familiar faces. Even her daughter Vicky looked as if she might race her mother to the grave. Victoria was old and frail, her eyesight was failing, her

Models of the marble effigies of Victoria and Albert, which lie over their sarcophagus at Frogmore.

rheumatism troublesome. Her nights were restless and her days consumed with compensating sleep. The shadow of war hung over the nation. Once again her 'dear soldiers' were fighting overseas in Africa where the clash between the Boers and the Uitlanders had led to war, a war which in its early stages was going badly for Britain. Yet, even here, there was some comfort to be found in that the Colonies sent expeditionary forces to help the Motherland. When reverses were at their worst, the Queen proudly declared 'there is no depression in this house'. Nevertheless she grieved for the slain, the bereaved, the wounded. In February 1900 the Queen visited the Herbert Hospital, touring the wards in her wheelchair, and presenting flowers to the wounded soldiers. To Victoria they were, in the words of the popular song, 'The Soldiers of the Queen'. Touched by the valour of the Irish regiments, in April she at last paid a long overdue visit to Ireland. During all the long years of her widowhood, though Victoria had spent many holidays abroad, she had never been to Ireland.

The Queen struggled on indomitably to the end of 1900, refusing to abandon her control of public business. But on New Year's Day, when it was her custom to take stock, she wrote that she felt so weak and unwell that she entered the new year sadly. Her zest for life had gone, but she was still doing some signing on 13 January. Then the journal, kept so faithfully since she had been thirteen, stopped. On the 19th a bulletin warned her subjects that the Queen was not in her usual health. On the 22nd, surrounded by her children and grandchildren, Victoria died. To the people of Britain the news of her death seemed the end of an era, as indeed it was. For the last time the crowds gathered in London, but this time there was no cheering and decorations, only a pall of sorrow and loss, as the funeral procession traversed London to Paddington Station, the starting place of so many of her journeys. Before her death, Victoria had left minute instructions for her funeral. In accordance with them her coffin, carried on a gun-carriage and covered with the royal standard, made its last journey to Frogmore. They laid her in the mausoleum, where so often as a broken-hearted widow she had sought strength and comfort. At last she was united with the man she had always loved and mourned so long. On the sarcophagus their marble effigies now lie side by side.

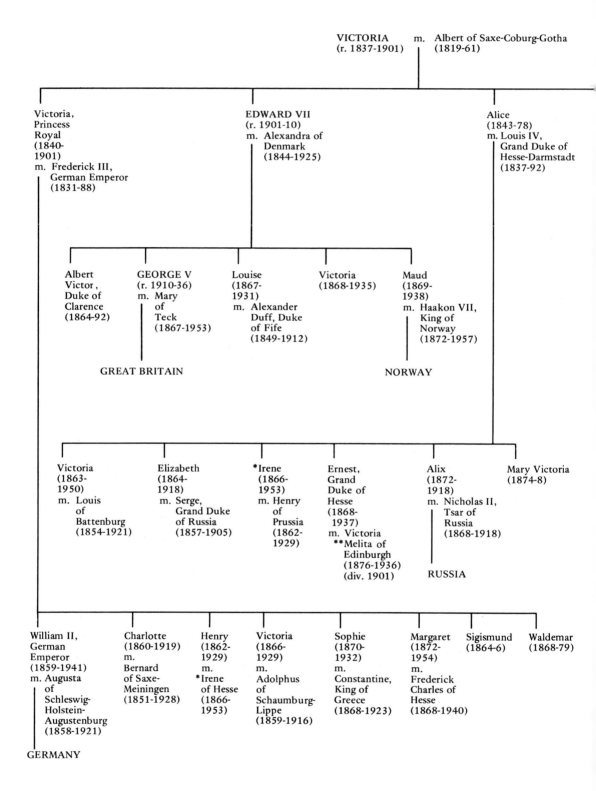

VICTORIA (r. 1837-1901) m. Albert of Saxe-Coburg-Gotha (1819-61)

Victoria, Princess Royal (1840-1901) m. Frederick III, German Emperor (1831-88)

EDWARD VII (r. 1901-10) m. Alexandra of Denmark (1844-1925)

Alice (1843-78) m. Louis IV, Grand Duke of Hesse-Darmstadt (1837-92)

Albert Victor, Duke of Clarence (1864-92)

GEORGE V (r. 1910-36) m. Mary of Teck (1867-1953)

Louise (1867-1931) m. Alexander Duff, Duke of Fife (1849-1912)

Victoria (1868-1935)

Maud (1869-1938) m. Haakon VII, King of Norway (1872-1957)

GREAT BRITAIN

NORWAY

Victoria (1863-1950) m. Louis of Battenburg (1854-1921)

Elizabeth (1864-1918) m. Serge, Grand Duke of Russia (1857-1905)

*Irene (1866-1953) m. Henry of Prussia (1862-1929)

Ernest, Grand Duke of Hesse (1868-1937) m. Victoria **Melita of Edinburgh (1876-1936) (div. 1901)

Alix (1872-1918) m. Nicholas II, Tsar of Russia (1868-1918)

RUSSIA

Mary Victoria (1874-8)

William II, German Emperor (1859-1941) m. Augusta of Schleswig-Holstein-Augustenburg (1858-1921)

GERMANY

Charlotte (1860-1919) m. Bernard of Saxe-Meiningen (1851-1928)

Henry (1862-1929) m. *Irene of Hesse (1866-1953)

Victoria (1866-1929) m. Adolphus of Schaumburg-Lippe (1859-1916)

Sophie (1870-1932) m. Constantine, King of Greece (1868-1923)

Margaret (1872-1954) m. Frederick Charles of Hesse (1868-1940)

Sigismund (1864-6)

Waldemar (1868-79)

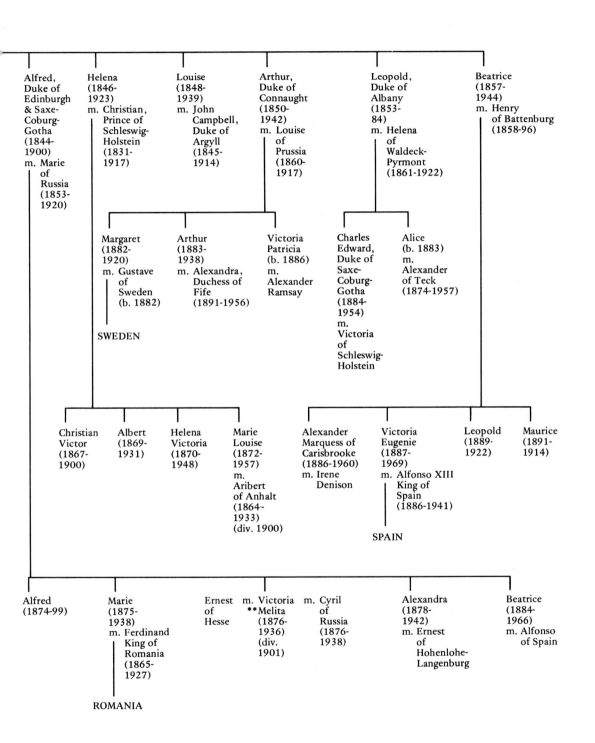

Alfred,
Duke of
Edinburgh
& Saxe-
Coburg-
Gotha
(1844-
1900)
m. Marie
of
Russia
(1853-
1920)

Helena
(1846-
1923)
m. Christian,
Prince of
Schleswig-
Holstein
(1831-
1917)

Louise
(1848-
1939)
m. John
Campbell,
Duke of
Argyll
(1845-
1914)

Arthur,
Duke of
Connaught
(1850-
1942)
m. Louise
of
Prussia
(1860-
1917)

Leopold,
Duke of
Albany
(1853-
84)
m. Helena
of
Waldeck-
Pyrmont
(1861-1922)

Beatrice
(1857-
1944)
m. Henry
of Battenburg
(1858-96)

Margaret
(1882-
1920)
m. Gustave
of
Sweden
(b. 1882)

SWEDEN

Arthur
(1883-
1938)
m. Alexandra,
Duchess of
Fife
(1891-1956)

Victoria
Patricia
(b. 1886)
m.
Alexander
Ramsay

Charles
Edward,
Duke of
Saxe-
Coburg-
Gotha
(1884-
1954)
m.
Victoria
of
Schleswig-
Holstein

Alice
(b. 1883)
m.
Alexander
of Teck
(1874-1957)

Christian
Victor
(1867-
1900)

Albert
(1869-
1931)

Helena
Victoria
(1870-
1948)

Marie
Louise
(1872-
1957)
m.
Aribert
of Anhalt
(1864-
1933)
(div. 1900)

Alexander
Marquess of
Carisbrooke
(1886-1960)
m. Irene
Denison

Victoria
Eugenie
(1887-
1969)
m. Alfonso XIII
King of
Spain
(1886-1941)

SPAIN

Leopold
(1889-
1922)

Maurice
(1891-
1914)

Alfred
(1874-99)

Marie
(1875-
1938)
m. Ferdinand
King of
Romania
(1865-
1927)

ROMANIA

Ernest
of
Hesse

m. Victoria
**Melita
(1876-
1936)
(div.
1901)

m. Cyril
of
Russia
(1876-
1938)

Alexandra
(1878-
1942)
m. Ernest
of
Hohenlohe-
Langenburg

Beatrice
(1884-
1966)
m. Alfonso
of Spain

Select bibliography

ORIGINAL MATERIAL

The Girlhood of Queen Victoria (1912)

The Letters of Queen Victoria, ed. A. C. Benson, Viscount Esher and G. E. Buckle
  1st series 1837–61 (1907)
  2nd series 1861/2–85 (1926–8)
  3rd series 1886–1901 (1930–2)

Dearest Child: Letters between Queen Victoria and the Crown Princess of Prussia 1858–1861, ed. R. Fulford (1964)

Dearest Mama: Letters between Queen Victoria and the Crown Princess of Prussia 1861–1864, ed. R. Fulford (1968)

Your Dear Letter: Private Correspondence of Queen Victoria and the Crown Princess of Prussia 1865–1871 (1971)

Darling Child: Private Correspondence of Queen Victoria and the Crown Princess of Prussia 1871–1878, ed. R. Fulford (1976)

Beloved Mama: Private Correspondence of Queen Victoria and the German Crown Princess 1878–1885, ed. R. Fulford (1981)

Queen Victoria in her Letters and Journals: A Selection, ed. C. Hibbert (1984)

Advice to a Grand-daughter: Letters from Queen Victoria to Princess Victoria of Hesse, selected with a commentary by Richard Hough (1975)

Victoria Travels: Journeys of Queen Victoria between 1830 and 1900, with extracts from her Journal (1970)

Our Life in the Highlands, by Queen Victoria (1868)

Queen Victoria's Highland Journals, ed. D. Duff (1980)

BIOGRAPHIES

Blake, R., *Disraeli* (1966)

Bolitho, H., *The Reign of Queen Victoria* (1949)
  The Prince Consort (1964)

Cecil, David, *Lord M.* (1954)

HRH The Duchess of York with Benita Stoney, *Victoria and Albert: Life at Osborne House* (1991)

Duff, D., *Albert and Victoria* (1972)

Epton, Nina, *Victoria and Her Daughter* (1971)

Fulford, R., *Queen Victoria* (1951)
  The Prince Consort (1949)

Hobhouse, Hermione, *Prince Albert: His Life and Work* (1983)

James, Robert Rhodes, *Albert, Prince Consort: A Biography* (1983)

Longford, Elizabeth, *Victoria RI* (1964)

Magnus, P., *King Edward VII* (1964)
  Gladstone: A Biography (1954)

Mullen, Richard, and Munson, James, *Victoria: Portrait of a Queen* (1987)

Plowden, Alison, *Young Victoria* (1981)

Richardson, Joanna, *Victoria and Albert* (1977)

Shearman, Deidre, *Queen Victoria* (1990)

Sitwell, Edith, *Victoria of England* (1936)

Strachey, Lytton, *Queen Victoria* (1921)
  The Illustrated Queen Victoria (1987)

Thompson, Dorothy, *Queen Victoria: Gender and Power* (1990)

Weintraub, Stanley, *Victoria: Biography of a Queen* (1987)

Whittle, Tyler, *Victoria and Albert at Home* (1980)

Woodham-Smith, Cecil, *Queen Victoria: Her Life and Times. Vol I: 1819–1861* (1972)

BACKGROUND BOOKS

Aronson, T., *Grandmama of Europe: The Crowned Descendants of Queen Victoria* (1973)

Cecil, Algernon, *Queen Victoria and Her Prime Ministers*

Chadwick, Owen, *Victorian Miniature* (1960)

Clark, G. Kitson, *The Making of Victorian England* (1962)

Ensor, R. C. K., *England 1870–1914* (1936)

Lane, Peter, *The Victorian Age 1830–1914* (1972)

Laver, J., *Victorian Vista* (1954)

Nevill, Barry St John, *Life at the Court of Queen Victoria 1861–1901* (1984)

Priestley, J. B., *Victoria's Heyday* (1972)

Reader, William Joseph, *Life in Victorian England* (rev. ed., 1985)

Sansom, William, *Victorian Life in Photographs* (rev. ed., 1974)

Thompson, F. M. L., *The Rise of Respectable Society: A Social History of Victorian Britain 1830–1900* (1988)

Woodward, E. L., *The Age of Reform 1815–1870* (1938)

Young, G. M., ed., *Early Victorian England 1830–1865*, 2 vols (1934)
  Victorian England: The Portrait of an Age (1936)

Index